"Spectacular and exhilarating, but also inaccessible—John Owen can be like that. His view of the triune God is glorious, yet reading Owen is like climbing a mountain. But just as you can take a helicopter tour to see the marvels of a mountain range, so Mike McKinley lifts us up into Owen's thoughts with easy-to-understand explanations to see the wonders of knowing the Father, the Son, and the Holy Spirit. This book will greatly help many fellowship more fully with God, whose friendship, in Christ, is more than a brother's. Highly recommended for all believers yearning to have a closer and richer life with each of the persons of the Trinity!"

Joel R. Beeke, President, Puritan Reformed Theological Seminary

"Probably no book has influenced my theological instincts more than John Owen's *Communion with God*, but Owen is not always easy to read. Therefore, this small volume by Mike McKinley is a welcome gift. He ably conveys in an accessible and friendly way many of Owen's key ideas from that book, inviting readers to consider the kindness of the God who desires to be in communion with us."

Kelly M. Kapic, Professor of Theological Studies, Covenant College

"While thoughtful Christians will know that the doctrine of the Trinity is biblically true, fewer see it as the fountain of their entire Christian spirituality. But Mike McKinley ably shows how the triune God invites the believer into a deeply nuanced threefold relationship—a friendship even—with Father, Son, and Holy Spirit. In McKinley's capable hands, John Owen's original (dense!) writing on these themes opens up and breathes, inviting every reader into the Trinitarian depths."

Brian Kay, Pastor of Christian Formation, Walnut Creek Presbyterian Church, Walnut Creek, California; author, *Trinitarian Spirituality: John Owen and the Doctrine of God in Western Devotion*

"John Owen's *Communion with God* proves that this titan of English theology was also a sensitive pastor and guide who wanted his listeners and readers to love the triune God fervently. Yet Owen's style is complex and can be difficult for modern readers. Enter Mike McKinley, himself a seasoned pastor, who in this short book synthesizes much of the gist of Owen's treatise. Full of choice quotes from Owen, trenchant observations, and provocative questions, McKinley's overview will spur you on to communion, and indeed fellowship and friendship, with God!"

Shawn D. Wright, Professor of Church History, The Southern Baptist Theological Seminary; coeditor, *The Complete Works of John Owen*

Friendship with God

Friendship with God

*A Path to Deeper Fellowship with
the Father, Son, and Spirit*

Mike McKinley

WHEATON, ILLINOIS

Friendship with God: A Path to Deeper Fellowship with the Father, Son, and Spirit

Copyright © 2023 by Mike McKinley

Published by Crossway
1300 Crescent Street
Wheaton, Illinois 60187

Cover image and design: Faceout Studio, Spencer Fuller

First printing 2023

Printed in Colombia

Hardcover ISBN: 978-1-4335-8415-2
ePub ISBN: 978-1-4335-8418-3
PDF ISBN: 978-1-4335-8416-9

Library of Congress Cataloging-in-Publication Data

Names: McKinley, Mike, 1975– author.
Title: Friendship with God : a path to deeper fellowship with the Father, Son, and Spirit / Mike McKinley.
Description: Wheaton, Illinois : Crossway, 2023. | Includes bibliographical references and index.
Identifiers: LCCN 2022022674 (print) | LCCN 2022022675 (ebook) | ISBN 9781433584152 (hardcover) | ISBN 9781433584169 (pdf) | ISBN 9781433584183 (epub)
Subjects: LCSH: Owen, John, 1616–1683. Communion with the Triune God. | Spirituality—Christianity.
Classification: LCC BV4501.3 .O93 2023 (print) | LCC BV4501.3 (ebook) | DDC 248.4—dc23/eng/20221125
LC record available at https://lccn.loc.gov/2022022674
LC ebook record available at https://lccn.loc.gov/2022022675

Crossway is a publishing ministry of Good News Publishers.

NP		32	31	30	29	28	27	26	25	24	23
15	14	13	12	11	10	9	8	7	6	5	4	3	2	1

For the McCloths

Contents

Introduction

IMAGINE IF I TOLD YOU that I was friends with a lot of famous people: Dwayne "The Rock" Johnson, Jeff Bezos, Oprah Winfrey, and Taylor Swift (if it's easier for you, you can insert your own list of wealthy, impressive, important, powerful people). What if I told you that I am not only friendly with those people but that they all go to great lengths to be friends with me—they come to visit me all the time, they always pick up the phone when I call, and I have an open invitation to use their vacation homes and drive their sports cars whenever I'd like? You'd think I was a really big deal, wouldn't you? In fact, you would probably be more than a little envious of me. You might wonder what made me so special that people like that wanted to know me so well.

Well, if you are a Christian, the Bible says that the eternal God—the one who made the universe and everything in it, the God who is more holy and glorious and powerful than we can even begin to understand—*that* God wants you to know him and be known by him. He has gone to great lengths to make it possible for you to be his friend. He delights in your company and loves to shower you with good gifts. In fact, he plans to spend eternity blessing you far beyond what you can imagine. Just look at some of the ways the Bible describes our relationship to God:

- We are called his *friends* (e.g., Ps. 25:4; John 15:13–14)
- We are *in fellowship* with him (e.g., 1 Cor. 1:9; 1 John 1:3)
- We are *adopted* into his family (e.g., Rom. 8:23; Eph. 1:5)
- We are so connected to Jesus that we are his *body* (e.g., 1 Cor. 12:27; Eph. 5:29–30)
- We are even referred to as his *bride* (e.g., Isa. 54:5; Rev. 19:6–9)

That's pretty clear, isn't it? God intends to have a close and intimate connection with us.

At this point, however, I think Christians run into one of two problems. The first is that we find it hard to believe; it's simply too good to be true. If LeBron James left me a voicemail inviting me over to his house to shoot hoops and take a dip in his pool, I would assume that one of my buddies was playing a prank on me. There's nothing so special about me that I'd rate an invitation like that. I'm not the kind of person who sips drinks poolside with famous people.

In an even greater way, Christians might struggle to imagine that God would actually want to be friends with us. We have been given faith to believe that he has saved us from our sin and provided us with eternal life in Christ, and honestly that's far beyond what we have a right to expect. But the idea that he wants even more for us, that he wants to be in a close relationship with us? That all seems like a bit much.

The second difficulty that Christians run into is that it can be hard to know what it means, practically speaking, to have a friendship with God. When we become followers of Christ, someone usually gives us some sense of what to do next: go to church, avoid sin, read the Bible, and pray. That's a really good plan, and we would all do well to follow it. But the question is, What does any of that have to do with being God's friend? More than that, what does it even mean to have a relationship with God? Is it some kind of sense of a "spiritual" feeling? Is it an emotional experience that we are supposed to get while singing in church? Is it some new insight into God and his ways?

I know both of those struggles, in my own life and in the lives of the brothers and sisters in the church I pastor. I see it in the Christians who leave to find another church that makes them feel "more spiritual," in those who are always looking for the new conference or program that will unlock the key insight they need to feel closer to God, in those who have grown doubtful that God could really love someone like them, in those who feel like their walk with the Lord has simply stalled out, and in the people who have settled into going through the motions, hoping that something will change someday.

If you can identify at all with either of these difficulties, I've written this book to introduce you to some ideas that I have found to be enormously eye-opening. To be clear, they aren't new ideas, and they aren't mine. They come from *Communion with God*, a book written by an old English pastor named John Owen.

Owen's book started out as a series of sermons preached to teenagers at Oxford University in the early 1650s. In it, he uses the Scriptures to guide the reader into heartfelt fellowship with God the Father, Son, and Holy Spirit. It is full to the brim with truths about God and practical wisdom about how we ought live in light of them. I don't think I've ever read a book that helped me more (except, of course, the Bible).

The problem (and the reason for this book) is that Owen can be difficult to read and understand. His language is outdated, the world that he was writing to is very different from ours, he never tires of listing out points and subpoints, and his writing style can seem overly complicated at times (he never seems to explain anything in ten words if he can explain it in fifty!). As a result, *Communion with God* just isn't something that most twenty-first-century Christians are going to pick up and read.

My goal in this little book is to mine some of the most precious diamonds of Owen's spiritual insights and make them available and applicable to you as you grow in your enjoyment of the friendship of the God who is Father, Son, and Holy Spirit. I've tried to provide some of Owen's most accessible and helpful quotes from the book, and if this motivates you to go read Owen on your own, you will be richly rewarded for your time and effort. It is true that some wonderful things are inevitably lost when you take a masterpiece written by a genius and let a (definite) nongenius like me shorten, rephrase, and rework it. But while some of Owen's brilliance has certainly been lost in the process of creating this book, I do have hope that much good remains to serve you in your friendship with God.

It has been my earnest prayer that this book will be helpful to you. Or, as John Owen put it in the preface to *Communion*, "know only that the whole of it has been recommended to the grace of God in many supplications, for its usefulness unto them that are interested in the good things mentioned therein."[1] (See, I told you he was wordy!)

On that note, let's get started.

---

[1] All citations from Owen's original work, *Communion with God*, are taken from a helpful contemporary edition, *Communion with the Triune God*, ed. Kelly M. Kapic and Justin Taylor (Wheaton, IL: Crossway, 2007), 86.

PART 1

_____

COMMUNION WITH THE TRIUNE GOD

1

Saved for Communion

FRIENDSHIPS FORM when two people value each other, care about each other, and want to spend time together. If only one person in a relationship cares about the other and wants to spend time together, you don't have a friendship—you just have an awkward, uncomfortable situation. If you've ever been in a relationship like that, where you cared more and gave more of yourself than the other person, you know how painful it can be. Friendship is meant to be a two-way street; otherwise it's not really friendship.

And that raises a problem for us when it comes to our fellowship with God, because we aren't naturally his friends. We aren't born loving God and his ways; we don't wake up every morning thinking of him and wanting to know him and please him and spend time with him. Instead, we go about our lives thinking about ourselves. We focus on the things we have and the things we want to have. We mistreat other people, tell lies, and squander the talents and opportunities God has given us. We take the things God has given to us and use them to make other things more important than he is. I don't even have to know you to know that all of that is true of you, because it's true of all of us.

As a result, the Bible describes human beings as God's enemies (Rom. 5:10), as being spiritually "dead" (Eph. 2:1), "haters of God" (Rom. 1:30), and "children of wrath" (Eph. 2:3). That's about as far away from friendship with God as we could possibly be! So the first question we must answer is this: How can people *like us* become friends with someone *like God*? We have offended him and rejected him. We've made ourselves his opponents. How could we possibly be his friend, even if we wanted to?

The answer to that question seems clear: we can't! It is impossible for you and me to be in a good relationship with God, just like a criminal can't enjoy the company of a police officer, and the employee who has been embezzling money from his company doesn't look forward to a long, leisurely dinner with his boss. Friendship with God is simply impossible—unless God himself makes it happen. He must act. He must do something to mend our relationship. All the cards are in his hands. He is the judge; we are the condemned. He is the king; we are the traitors. He is the faithful spouse; we are the cheaters. If God doesn't break through our rebellion and hatred and do something to restore us to him, we are lost.

The message of Christianity is that this is exactly what our God has done for us. In his great love for people like you and me, God the Father sent his Son to become a man, to die for our sins on the cross, and to rise from the dead in victory over everything that keeps us from being in a good relationship with him. When the risen Jesus ascended into heaven, he sent God the Holy Spirit to give us new spiritual lives and comfort and help us. God has done everything that needed to be done for us to be his friends. Jesus removed the sin and guilt of everyone who puts their trust in him, so now we are welcomed into the family. We are now spiritually united to Jesus, and what he has is now ours as well. Jesus is holy, so we are considered holy in God's sight. Jesus is pleasing to God, so we are pleasing to him as well.

And here's the thing you must understand, or else everything is going to get off track: you can't mess that up. Because you didn't do anything to make yourself God's friend, you can't do anything to break that relationship. If you have put your faith in Jesus, you are spiritually connected to him. Your status before God doesn't depend on your performance or work or obedience; it depends on Jesus, and he did everything perfectly in order to make you God's friend. Nothing can ever separate you from God's love in Christ (Rom. 8:38–39). Once he has made you his friend through faith in Jesus, you can never be his enemy again.

It is important to be crystal clear on this fact: our status as God's friends has nothing to do with anything good or bad that we do. It comes to us as a gift, not because we have obeyed God and loved him, but because he chose to love us. God has done all the work. He thought of the idea, he did everything that needed to be done, and he paid every price that needed to be paid. We contribute nothing to the process; we simply receive our new identity as God's friends through faith in Christ.

Because this is true, when we talk about friendship with God in this book (or, to use John Owen's word, our *communion* with God) we are talking about something different from that new status we have in Christ. We are talking instead about our daily *awareness*, *experience*, and *enjoyment* of that new status. This is the part where we come in, where we play a role and have work to do. Our *union* with God is a gift we are given; we don't do anything except receive it by faith. Our *communion* with God, however, is like any other friendship; it is an active, two-way relationship.

Here's how Owen explained what it means to have this kind of back-and-forth friendship with God: "Our communion, then, with God consists in his *communication of himself unto us, with our return unto him* of that which he requires and accepts, flowing from that *union* which in Jesus Christ we have with him."[1]

In that last phrase, Owen says that our *communion* flows from our *union* with Jesus. Or, we might say, we have a *friendship* with God because we have been made his *friends* in Jesus. Because we are in Jesus and the Holy Spirit lives in us, we have a lot in common with God now. Like any friendship, we love the same things our friend loves, and we delight in the things that please him.

This communion is a two-way street. God (in Owen's words) communicates of himself unto us. Like a friend, he talks to us and reveals himself to us and shows us who he is and what makes him tick. And like any friend, Christians are able to "return" something to God. He has given us some specific ways to communicate our friendship back to him, things like prayer, love, delight, obedience, and participation in the Lord's Supper. Owen calls them "that which he requires and accepts," and our role in the friendship is to pursue intimacy with God, knowledge of God, and love for God through those means. But that's a subject we will unpack more in future chapters. For now, the incredible news is

---

1 John Owen, *Communion with the Triune God*, ed. Kelly M. Kapic and Justin Taylor (Wheaton, IL: Crossway, 2007), 94. Unless otherwise noted, all emphases in Owen quotations are original.

that God wants you to experience friendship (or fellowship, or communion) with him.

In order for us to have a genuine friendship with God, we need to hold two truths in tension. The first is that God is incredibly holy and powerful. He is "a consuming fire" (Heb. 12:29) and a glorious King (Ps. 24:8); he is so mighty and beautiful that you would never think of getting anywhere near him. In fact, when people in the Bible do get anywhere near him, they tend to freak out (e.g., Ex. 19:16; Isa. 6:5; Luke 5:8). You would never dare to approach someone like him in friendship unless you were sure that he wanted you to. You'd be far too terrified to get close to anyone so mighty and pure, unless you were 100 percent confident that he loves you, delights in you, and is smiling on you.

The amazing discovery of the gospel, the good news that we would never dare to believe if God hadn't said it, is that when we draw near to God, we find not anger at our failures and sins but sympathy, mercy, and grace to help us in our time of need (Heb. 4:15–16). That's the second of the two truths we must hold together.

Think for a second about what it is like to sit down and spend time with a good friend. You aren't constantly worried about what you are going to talk about and whether you might accidentally offend him by saying the wrong thing. You are not concerned that he will reject you if you share your weaknesses, fears, and failures; in fact, you share those things with him in the confidence that he will help you bear those burdens. There's no concern that he might be harboring a grudge or secretly merely tolerating you. There's an ease, a comfort, and a boldness in true friendship. Both parties know that the other one loves them. God has given you friends like that on earth so that you will have a small taste of what it means to have a relationship with him, so that you will have some pale experience of what it is like to have a perfect friend like him.

A one-sided relationship isn't much of a friendship. We might be tempted to think that people like us could never love and be loved by a holy God. But perhaps we could say that the very first step toward enjoying friendship with God is to realize that he wants you to be his friend.

2

Friendship with the Three in One

WHEN YOU THINK ABOUT GOD, what images come to your mind? Do you think of him as a great king? A mighty creator? A righteous judge? A loving protector? All those things are true and easily demonstrated from the Bible, but none of those conceptions of God is uniquely Christian; a Muslim or Jewish or Mormon friend would probably agree with all of them.

As we think about friendship with God, we want to make sure that we are pursuing a relationship with the God of the Bible, the true God who really exists. And that means our communion is with the *triune* God. The Bible teaches us that the one true God exists eternally in three fully divine persons—the Father, the Son, and the Holy Spirit. Since that is the case, any *real* relationship with God must be carried on directly and distinctly with each of those three persons. That is to say, Christians can and must have direct fellowship with God the Father, God the Son, and God the Spirit.

You cannot be friends with someone unless you know him, and to know God is to know him as three persons in one. You can't accurately conceive of God without thinking of the three persons, and to think about each of the three persons inevitably brings you back to thinking about the unity of God. To help make this point, Owen refers to the words of one of the ancient church fathers, Gregory of Nazianzus, saying: "No sooner do I conceive of the One than I am illumined by the splendor of the Three; no sooner do I distinguish Them than I am carried back to the One."[1]

I want to show you from the Bible that this is true, because if it is, then there is hardly anything more important that we could say on the topic of friendship with God. Remember that we have already seen, in the previous chapter, that communion with God consists in his communication of himself to us and our response to him through the means that he has established. Just like our human friendships depend on our being willing to let ourselves be known, so our relationship with God depends on his willingness to let us know what he is like, what pleases him, and what he is doing in the world.

And when we turn to the Scriptures, we see that each person of the Trinity communicates directly with us in just that way. Owen demonstrates this truth using the promise that Jesus makes in John's Gospel: "It is written in the Prophets, 'And they will all be taught by God'" (John 6:45). According to Owen, that idea of being taught by God is right at the heart of friendship with him. He writes, "The teaching of God is the real communication of all and every particular emanation from himself unto the saints whereof they are made partakers."[2] That is to say, when Jesus

---

1 John Owen, *Communion with the Triune God*, ed. Kelly M. Kapic and Justin Taylor (Wheaton, IL: Crossway, 2007), 95n2.

2 Owen, *Communion*, 102.

promises us that we will be "taught by God," he is promising us that God will communicate with us about himself in ways that bring believers into a loving relationship with him.

Each person of the Trinity is involved in fulfilling Jesus's promise by teaching God's people.

- *God the Father.* In the same verse that Owen quotes (John 6:45), Jesus speaks of his people as those who have "learned from the Father." He says, "Everyone who has heard and learned from the Father comes to me."

- *God the Son.* God the Father tells us to listen to his Son (Matt. 17:5), and throughout his earthly ministry the Lord Jesus taught his followers to know him and his ways: "No longer do I call you servants, for the servant does not know what his master is doing; but I have called you friends, for all that I have heard from my Father I have made known to you" (John 15:15).

- *God the Spirit.* The Holy Spirit reveals, instructs, and enlightens the mind of believers so that we can know God: "The Helper, the Holy Spirit, whom the Father will send in my name, he will teach you all things and bring to your remembrance all that I have said to you" (John 14:26).

There is a big difference between knowing a lot about someone and actually knowing him as a friend. My hero growing up was Don Mattingly, the first baseman for the New York Yankees in the 1980s. I know a lot about him off the top of my head.

Without looking it up on the Internet, I can tell you his middle name (Arthur), his birthday (April 20), and his place of birth (Evanston, Illinois). But I don't really know him—I don't know much about his personality or what he's like when he's at home or what makes him happy. He doesn't call to let me know about his plans; he doesn't confide in me about his feelings. While I know things about him, I can't actually say that I *know* him as a friend.

Knowing God as a friend is far more complex than knowing any human being, and God is far more exalted than any human being we might admire. So we find ourselves completely dependent on God's willingness to teach us about himself. Otherwise we will only ever know him at a great distance (with the kind of knowledge of God as described in Romans 1:19–21). But in his love for us, God has stooped down to reveal himself to us as he truly is—Father, Son, and Holy Spirit—so that we can really know him. We will never know everything there is to know about God; he is too great, and we are finite. But we can know him truly, because God the Father teaches us by sending his Son, by giving us the Bible, and by illuminating our understanding through the work of the Holy Spirit inside every believer. Through those means God doesn't merely teach us information about himself but genuinely causes us to know him as a friend.

One of the great joys of the Christian life is reading God's word (or hearing it preached) with a clear and growing sense that the Creator of the universe, who holds all things in his hand, is speaking directly to you as his friend. But as we've said, a friendship is a two-way street; we have to do something with God's loving communication of himself. Here's what Owen says about our part in having a relationship with God:

The way and means, then, on the part of the saints, whereby in Christ they enjoy communion with God, are all the spiritual and holy actings and outgoings of their souls in those graces, and by those ways, wherein both the *moral* and *instituted* worship of God doth consist. Faith, love, trust, joy, etc., are the natural or moral worship of God, whereby those in whom they are have communion with him.[3]

If Owen is correct (and I believe he is, since he is accurately reflecting the Bible's teaching), then this is very good news for us. We are not left to guess how we are supposed to conduct a friendship with God. If you are a Christian, you do not have to wait around for some profound spiritual experience to suddenly take over you. You don't need to be a monk or a guru or someone with some deep, special insight into the mysteries of the spiritual world. God knows that we wouldn't know how to have communion with someone as awesome and holy and powerful as him, and so he's established and promises to bless a certain "way and means" (to use Owen's phrase) to worship him, to communicate our friendship back to him.

There's what Owen calls "natural" or "moral" worship, which includes things like faith, love, trust, and joy. These are things that you can experience during your normal day-to-day life. When you trust the Lord in a difficult situation, when you believe what he says in his word, when you feel love for him and joy in your salvation—that's communion with God. That's you acting like God's friend.

3 Owen, *Communion*, 97.

There's also what Owen calls "instituted" worship, which includes things like baptism, the Lord's Supper, songs of praise, prayer, and the preaching of the Bible. These are things God has called his people to participate in during their church gatherings so that they can respond to his word and communicate back to him their love, faith, and joy.

The amazing reality at the heart of Owen's book is that we can have this kind of communion and direct friendship with each person of the Trinity. If you are in Christ, you are loved by the Father, Son, and Holy Spirit, and each one of those persons has ways of communicating love and grace to you. And in response, you have the wonderful privilege of loving, praying to, praising, believing, trusting, and rejoicing directly in all three persons.

PART 2

———————

COMMUNION WITH
THE FATHER

3

A Loving Father

IF WE WHAT SAW in the previous chapter is true—that we can have communion with each of the three persons of the Trinity directly—then it's worth asking how our communion with God the Father might be different from our communion with God the Son and God the Holy Spirit. To help us understand what those relationships should look like, Owen uses the word *medium* to describe what is unique in our friendship with each person of the Trinity.

As Owen intends it, a *medium* is the thing through which a relationship is carried out. For example, we might say that the medium of your relationship with your dentist is your teeth. She addresses any problem there might be with your teeth, and you pay her gladly for her services. When you see your dentist, your teeth are the main topic of conversation; in fact, they are the thing that brings you together. You might chat with her about sports or the weather, but when it comes down to it, yours is a tooth-mediated relationship.[1]

---

1 I'm indebted to Brian Kay for his clear explanation of Owen's use of *medium* in his book *Trinitarian Spirituality: John Owen and the Doctrine of God in Western Devotion* (Milton Keynes, UK: Paternoster Press, 2007), 124–25.

Owen wants us to see that in the Bible's communication of the gospel message to us, there is a specific medium by which we have a relationship with God the Father, a different specific medium by which we conduct our relationship with God the Son, and yet another medium by which we relate to God the Holy Spirit. Those are the things that we will be examining and unpacking as we go through this book. So at the outset, Owen wants us to see that the medium of our friendship with God the Father is *love*. He writes:

> I come now to declare what it is wherein peculiarly and eminently the saints have communion with the Father; and this is *love*—free, undeserved, and eternal love. This the Father peculiarly fixes upon the saints; this they are immediately to eye in him, to receive of him, and to make such returns thereof as he is delighted withal. This is the great *discovery* of the gospel.[2]

Love stands at the center of your friendship with God the Father. Your teeth create your relationship to your dentist; your car is the foundation of your dealings with your auto mechanic. But when we "do business" with God the Father, love takes center stage. Before we go any further, just think about how wonderful that is, that the Father has not centered his friendship with you on the concept of his justice or his power or his law. Those are all good things, but they would make a friendship with God very frightening indeed. When God the Father relates to you, he does so through his love. That is the main topic he wants to talk to

2 John Owen, *Communion with the Triune God*, ed. Kelly M. Kapic and Justin Taylor (Wheaton, IL: Crossway, 2007), 107.

you about. That's what he wants you to think of when you think about him.

Now, that might be hard for you to believe. Perhaps you think that God's justice or his holiness or his law stand as the medium of your relationship. If you do, then you probably think that what God really wants to talk about with you is your obedience, your sin, and all the rules you need to keep. And if that's the case, I would expect that you do not enjoy your relationship with the Father all that much. Owen admits that for this very reason, "Christians walk oftentimes with exceedingly troubled hearts, concerning the thoughts of the Father toward them."[3]

But a Christian should never doubt the love of the Father for him, for love touches on the heart of who the Father is. In 1 John 4:8 we read that "God is love." We know that the apostle John is speaking specifically about God the Father there, for just a bit later he tells us: "In this the love of God was made manifest among us, that God sent his only Son into the world, so that we might live through him" (1 John 4:9). When John says that "God is love," he is referring specifically to God the Father, the one who showed his love by sending his Son into the world for us.

So while, of course, God the Son and God the Spirit are also loving, the Bible singles out love as the way we particularly relate to God the Father (see, for example, 2 Corinthians 13:14). It is the love of God the Father that motivated him to send his Son into the world in order to save sinners (John 3:16), and it is the love of the Father that is referred to in Romans 5:5, when the

3   Owen, *Communion*, 110.

apostle Paul writes, "God's love has been poured into our hearts through the Holy Spirit who has been given to us."

The Father's love is a beautiful thing, far more wonderful than any other love we might know. This love serves as a foundation for all the good things the Father has done for us, and it is capable of transforming the person who has received it. This love springs up from the Father's nature, so he does not need us to be worthy of love before he loves us (Rom. 5:8). Because he is perfect, his love can never change; it does not shrink or grow. He loves all his children with the exact same intensity and passion.

The good news is that God the Father relates to us in love. But what is our part? Remember that any friendship is a two-way street; if God the Father loves us, then what should we do in response? What is our role in the relationship? Owen suggests two things: we must first receive God's love and then we must "make suitable returns unto him."[4] Let's look at the first of those two ideas in the rest of this chapter, and then we can consider the second in the next.

In order to have a relationship with the Father, we must receive his love. Friendship is a give-and-take, so we must be willing to "take" the Father's love by faith. Now, hang with me here, because we need to take a small step back to understand what that means. The faith required of us is primarily faith in God the Son, and it is through him that we come to the Father and are convinced of his love (John 14:6). Jesus leads us by the hand, so to speak, and brings us into the Father's presence, where we experience his love. Owen writes, "Though the saints may, nay, *do* see an infinite ocean

---

4   Owen, *Communion*, 111.

of love unto them in the bosom of the Father, yet they are not to look for one drop from him but what comes through Christ."[5]

Owen employs a word picture to help us understand what this looks like. Imagine you are drinking from a cool, clear stream of running water. The water you are enjoying, the refreshment you are receiving, actually has its source in a spring far away. The stream is the means by which we experience the benefits of the spring; it brings them to you so that you can enjoy them. In the same way, the love of God is like that spring or fountain far away, and Jesus is like a stream that brings that love to us. Owen writes, comparing Jesus to both a beam of light and a stream of water: "Jesus Christ, in respect of the love of the Father, is but the beam, the stream; wherein though actually all our light, our refreshment lies, yet by him we are led to the fountain, the sun of eternal love itself."[6] We receive the Father's love through faith in Jesus, by believing the good news that the Father loved us so much that he sent his Son to save us and bring us into his presence.

The Father wants you to know him as he truly is—"benign, kind, tender, loving"—but sadly "few can carry up their hearts and minds to this height by faith, as to rest their souls in the love of the Father."[7] If you do not rest in the love of the Father, then your friendship with the Father will suffer. But we can learn to rest ourselves more fully in his love and so experience his friendship more fully. If you are a Christian, you should work hard to convince yourself of the Father's love for you, revealed in the gift of his Son. Do not allow your sin or fear to cause you to doubt

5   Owen, *Communion*, 117.
6   Owen, *Communion*, 112.
7   Owen, *Communion*, 112.

his love for you; he never changes, so he will never stop loving you in Christ.

The Father wants to have a friendship with you, centered on his love. If he seems distant, or if your life is marked by spiritual turmoil and upset rather than rest, then this is where you must begin. Allow God's word to convince you of his love. Look to all that Jesus has done for you in his death and resurrection, and drink deeply from that stream of the Father's love. Fight hard against the unbelief and fear that would tempt you to believe he doesn't love you. We commune with the Father in his love.

4

The Father's Love and Ours

IN THE LAST CHAPTER we saw that God the Father loves us with a great and unchanging love. That is an incredible truth on which we can build our lives, our identity, and our hope for eternity. And we also saw that in order to have communion with the Father and enjoy a close sense of relationship with him, we must receive his love through faith in Christ. But that's not all—any good friendship is based both on receiving love and giving it back, and it is the same for our friendship with the Father. We must receive his love, and we also must love him in return.

So what does it look like to love the Father? Well, the Bible is clear that obedience is part of the way we love him: "For this is the love of God, that we keep his commandments" (1 John 5:3a). That might seem odd to us; how can love and obedience be related? We might be tempted to think that they are on opposite sides of the spectrum, as if love is a pleasant emotion while obedience is drudgery and a burden. But that very same verse in the Bible continues on to say, "And his commandments are not burdensome" (1 John 5:3b). When you see God's commands as the good pleasure of your loving heavenly Father rather than a series of harsh restrictions on your joy, it makes obedience a delight.

We experience this dynamic in our human relationships all the time. I do things that I know will please my wife (like occasionally bringing home flowers), and I avoid things that I know will displease her (like growing a mustache; she has an irrational hatred for mustaches). I don't do those things because I am afraid of her or because I am trying to earn her love. Rather, I do them (or don't do them) because I love her, and *it makes me happy to make her happy*. Most human friendships work this way without us feeling burdened in the slightest.

Our obedience to God works in a similar way. As our sovereign Creator, he certainly has the right simply to command and expect our obedience. But our heavenly Father wants more than that from us and for us. He wants us to obey him as our loving response to his love. When I'm tempted to sin and I refrain, I am not primarily motivated by fear of judgment (Jesus has already taken my judgment at the cross) or concern that I will lose God's love (nothing can separate me from his love for me in Christ Jesus, not even my sin). Instead, I am motivated by the knowledge that the Father loves me, that he only commands what is good for me, and that it pleases him when I follow his instructions.

This is difficult for some people to understand, especially if they don't have a relationship with God. We usually consider obedience in terms of punishment and force. I don't exceed the speed limit in my car because I don't want to be pulled over by the police and face the consequences. If you have never experienced the love of your heavenly Father, you are probably going to imagine that Christian obedience works the same way. And there's a certain logical sense to that way of thinking. After all, if God loves me when I sin and when I obey, why wouldn't I just choose to do whatever I want to do?

Now, some might object to the idea that the Father's love (and not the threat of punishment) is our greatest motivation to obedience. After all, if we don't have to worry about losing God's love, won't we feel free to sin as much we want? Owen answers in the strongest terms: "He never tasted of the love of God that can seriously make this objection. The *doctrine* of grace may be turned into wantonness [unrestrained sin]; the *principle* cannot."[1] That is to say, while some people can twist *the idea* of God's love into an excuse for sin, the real *experience* of God's love makes us want to please him rather than indulge our sinful desires. People who don't know the Father's unfailing and unshakable love might think that it would free us to do whatever we want to do, but those who have truly received it know that it makes us do whatever *he* wants us to do. When we return the Father's love with loving obedience, we are living out our friendship with God.

Obedience is an important way that Christians live out their love for their heavenly Father, but it might surprise you to learn that it is not the main event. Obedience is one of the responses that love for God produces in us, but it is not exactly the same thing as love itself. Instead, Owen says that "love is an affection of union and nearness, with complacency therein" and says that the love we return to the Father is "a peculiar delight and acquiescing in the Father."[2]

---

1 John Owen, *Communion with the Triune God*, ed. Kelly M. Kapic and Justin Taylor (Wheaton, IL: Crossway, 2007), 121.
2 Owen, *Communion*, 113, 114.

You see, our love for God the Father is something that takes place deep in our innermost person. Just look at the phrases that Owen uses to try to describe this love:

Affection of union and nearness. Our love involves a feeling of closeness to God. When you allow your mind to meditate on the truth of how the Father has loved you and how he has sent Christ to bring you near to him (check out Ephesians 2:4–7 and 2:17–19), it begins to impact how you feel. You will begin to have a real sense of just how God the Father has connected you to him by giving you the Holy Spirit and uniting you to Christ by faith.

Delight. Our love for the Father is rooted in just how wonderful his love for us is. When we see something truly marvelous (e.g., a waterfall, a rainbow, the Philadelphia Eagles winning Super Bowl LII), our souls spontaneously experience delight. It's not something we have to manufacture or figure out; this feature is standard equipment on every model of human being. In the same way, when we glimpse some tiny sliver of just how beautiful the Father is, how graciously he has treated us, how much he loves us, and all that he has prepared for us in Christ, our souls will naturally delight in him.

Complacency and *acquiescing.* Before we experience the love of the Father for us, our souls can have no rest. We cannot feel true peace when we are troubled by our sin and have a sense of how far we are from God; we never find what we are truly looking for. In that state, the best we can hope for is something that distracts us from the nagging sense that things are not as they should be. But when we experience the Father's love, our souls find true rest. There is nothing missing; we have found that thing for which we were created—a relationship with our God. We can stop frantically searching and finally rest in the Father's love.

Let's put some feet on these ideas and look at what we should do in light of all this. We know that God the Father loves us; this is the reality on which our friendship with him is based. Our part of the equation is to love him in return, and that love (along with the obedience that it always produces) can spring only from a heart that is convinced it is loved (take a look at 1 John 4:19). So Owen writes: "When the soul sees God, in his dispensation of love, to be love, to be infinitely lovely and loving, rests upon and delights in him as such, then has its communion with him in love."[3]

If you find that your love for God the Father is less than what it should be (and that is the case for all of us this side of heaven), then there is work for you to do. It's delightful work, to be sure, but it will still require intentional effort on your part. What you need to do is work hard to convince yourself that the Father loves you. Your job is to convince yourself—over and over, every day—that the Father has set his loving favor on you and that this love comes to you in Christ.

If we apply ourselves to that one assignment, then our love for him will follow naturally. So Christian, set yourself this task: read the Bible, listen to the sermons at your church, sing hymns,

3 Owen, *Communion*, 113.

pray, and take the Lord's Supper, all with an eye toward helping your soul to better understand and believe in the Father's incredible love for you. As you grow in faith in his love, your soul will delight and rest in him more and more. That's how we enjoy a friendship with God the Father!

5

What the Father's Children Do

WHAT DOES GOD REQUIRE OF YOU? What pleases him most to see in his children? What makes someone an excellent Christian?

Perhaps you'd say that what God wants to see is extreme self-control, like that of the monks in a monastery maintaining silence and intentionally living in poverty. Or perhaps you'd say that the kinds of Christians that please God most are the pastors. After all, they devote their lives to studying the Bible and teaching God's people. Or maybe it's the missionaries who leave everything to go and spend their lives in a dangerous place, bringing the gospel to the lost. Or you could say that it's the Christians who devote all their time to fighting to see justice done for oppressed and needy people, running orphanages and homeless shelters and things like that (Mic. 6:8).

All those are good ways to invest your life (actually, to be honest, the monk thing isn't a great idea), but none of them represent our most basic duty as God's children. Owen wants us to see that none of those things represent what all Christians are obligated to do as part of their service to God. Instead, our great responsibility is to pursue a relationship with God the Father in his love. What that means is that everything we have been thinking about in terms of having a friendship with God, where he loves you and you love him in return, you are not free to take or leave. It's not an optional program for God's children. Instead, it is your *solemn obligation* to pursue and enjoy fellowship with him.

Now, I understand why that might sound like bad news to you. We tend to think of duty and obligation in negative terms. It is my duty to pay my taxes every year. I am obligated to take my car for a safety inspection every twelve months. None of those things bring me the slightest fragment of joy. I would happily be released from those requirements for the rest of my life.

But if you think about it, we also have a category for duties that are pleasant or even lovely. For example, there is a very real way that being my daughter's father means I'm *obligated* to attend her college graduation. But that isn't a tiresome chore; it will be a source of great joy. In the same way, my relationship with my son means that I *must* attend the play in which he is acting in a lead role. But it is hardly a burden; I'll have a giant smile on my face the whole time.

Our friendship with God is meant to be that kind of duty, one that fills us with life and joy. But maybe, if you're being honest, the idea doesn't really conjure up a lot of excitement and delight in your heart. I know I find myself in that place sometimes. Well, if it's any encouragement to you, Christians in Owen's time had the same struggle. He writes, "This is a duty wherein it is most evident that Christians are but little exercised—namely, in holding immediate communion with the Father in love."[1]

Why is that the case? Why is it that we find ourselves so easily excited about things that will bring us joy only for a moment (your favorite team winning a game, a new album dropping, a night out with friends), but we sometimes find ourselves relatively unmoved by our relationship with God the Father? It is very likely that we place too much value on those short-term pleasures, but the bigger problem is that we don't really understand how amazing it is to enjoy a relationship with the Father. Owen describes our problem this way: "Unacquaintedness with our mercies, our privileges, is our sin as well as our trouble. . . . This makes us go heavily, when we might rejoice; and to be weak, where we might be strong in the Lord."[2]

If you find yourself less than thrilled by your duty to enjoy your relationship with God, Owen would say that your biggest problem is that you do not really understand the "mercies and privileges" that are yours as the Father's beloved child. Have you ever seen a small child open a gift, only to wind up playing excitedly with the bow that was on the package? The problem is that he doesn't understand the value of the gift he has received; he is unacquainted with just what it is that he has been given. We are just like that child when we find our souls thrilled by the prospect of a new superhero movie but relatively unmoved by communion with the Father.

So what do you do with the toddler who ignores the gift in order to play with the glittery ribbons? You draw his attention

---

1   John Owen, *Communion with the Triune God*, ed. Kelly M. Kapic and Justin Taylor (Wheaton, IL: Crossway, 2007), 123.
2   Owen, *Communion*, 123.

to the gift. You show him how great it is and give him a sense of all the things he can do with it. You help him to experience the joy of the gift he has received. That's what Owen does for us. He takes us by the hand and helps us to delight in all that we have in our friendship with the Father. To that end, he gives us five steps to properly appreciate all we have received.

First, *eye the Father as love.* To eye something is to fix your mind on it in order to understand it more deeply. Believers are to fill their thoughts with the greatness of God's love and kindness. Don't think of him as a stern and disapproving father who focuses only on your shortcomings. If you focus your mind primarily "on his terrible majesty, severity, and greatness,"[3] your spirit will not be delighted by him, and you will not feel drawn into friendship with him. Instead, you should let your mind think often of his everlasting tenderness and compassion toward you in Christ. If you really understood how much the Father loves you, you would be delighted to be in his presence often.

Second, *think about who it is that loves us.* The Father who loves us has always been perfectly satisfied and happy. He is excellent and perfect in every way, enjoying the fellowship of the Son and the Spirit from eternity past. We don't fill up anything lacking in him; he doesn't need us at all. That means that his love isn't selfish. It isn't aimed at getting something from us, but it is a love that seeks our good.

Third, *meditate on what kind of love the Father has for us.* Some kinds of love are better than others, and the love of the Father is perfect in every way. It is:

3   Owen, *Communion*, 124.

Eternal. The Father has loved us before the world was created. Before we were born or had done anything good or bad, he delighted in us. From all eternity the Father has had a plan to bring us into his everlasting happiness. Just the idea that he loves us like this should make us "rejoice before him with trembling."[4]

Free. God loves us because he wants to; it makes him happy to love us. If he only loved us to the extent that we deserve it, he would love us much less. And if he loved us because he was obligated to love us, it would make his love less wonderful. But the truth is better than we might dare to imagine—nothing outside of the Father causes him to love us. His love is absolutely free.

Unchangeable. Because his love is free, it is also unchangeable. Nothing is going to come along and dislodge us from his tender kindness. God never changes, so his love will never grow or shrink. This is the only kind of love the Father could have for us, because if his love could be turned away by our sin or folly, it would have happened a long time ago!

Distinguishing. The Father's love is specific. He doesn't set his love on mankind in general but rather on those whom he has chosen in Christ from before the world was created (Eph. 1:4). This should give you a sense of awe and humility, that God has passed over many of the great and wise people of the world and made you an object of his love.

4 Owen, *Communion*, 125.

Fourth, *eye God's love so as to receive it.* It does you no good to understand the depth and beauty of the Father's love unless you receive it by faith, unless you really believe that he loves you like this. As you read God's word or hear it preached, work hard to understand what it says about the Father's love for you and then embrace that truth by faith. When your sin or the weakness of your faith tempts you to doubt that he cares for you, smother the flames of unbelief by putting your trust in what God has told you about his great love.

Fifth and finally, *let the Father's love change your heart.* If the Father has loved you like this, how unkind and ungrateful not to love him in return! If you have any comprehension of just how much he loves you, you will certainly love him in return.

Think for a moment about how wonderful this is. The religions of the world put a heavy burden on their followers. They teach that we must please God with our service, our self-control, and our acts of outward devotion. But the Father does not need you to be anything in order to love you. He doesn't need your service (Acts 17:25) or your religious devotion (Ps. 50:9–15). Rather, the command he gives is a great source of joy, that we believe how deeply he loves us in Christ and then love him in return. It is our happy duty to have communion with the Father in his love.

PART 3

———————

COMMUNION
WITH THE SON

6

A Gracious Savior

HAVING LED US TO THINK through what it means to have a direct relationship with God the Father, Owen moves on to a consideration of the personal communion we have with God the Son. As we will see, Owen was a Christ-centered preacher and writer; he understood that Jesus is the only way to know God and that all the truth about God must be seen in and through Christ. As a result, Owen spends almost two-thirds of his book on the friendship we have with God the Son.

It is clear from the Bible that we are intended to have a close and intimate relationship with Jesus. Remember what Paul wrote to the church at Corinth: "God is faithful, by whom you were called into the fellowship of his Son, Jesus Christ our Lord" (1 Cor. 1:9). Or think about the significance of what Jesus says to the church in Laodicea: "Behold, I stand at the door and knock. If anyone hears my voice and opens the door, I will come in to him and eat with him, and he with me" (Rev. 3:20). That's a sign of friendship, right? The picture here is that Jesus wants to come in and share a meal with us. Meals are where relationships are made, enjoyed, strengthened, and celebrated. When we have dinner with friends, we sit at the table, linger well after the food has been eaten, and enjoy the company and fellowship of the people we love. That's how Jesus feels about you, and it's what he wants you to experience with him.

How exactly we go about having that experience of friendship with God the Son is a subject Owen discusses at length. And here we should remind ourselves of something we talked about back in chapter 3, the idea of a "medium." Every relationship has a *medium*, a thing that brings the two parties together and holds the relationship together. Owen went to great lengths to show us that we have communion with the Father through the medium of his love; now he is going to show us that we have communion with God the Son through the medium of his grace.

That word *grace* is common enough in church circles, but sometimes it can be tricky to pin down exactly what it means. Owen points out that it is used in three different ways, all of which apply to our relationship with Jesus.

First, *grace* can refer to someone's personal presence and appearance. We might say that people conduct themselves with "style and grace," meaning that they are poised, attractive, and controlled.

Second, *grace* can refer to our experience of unearned favor and acceptance. When the Persian king Xerxes I set his love on Esther, we are told that she found "grace and favor in his sight" (Est. 2:17). Paul is also using the word *grace* in this sense when he tells the church at Ephesus: "By grace you have been saved through faith. And this is not your own doing; it is the gift of God, not a result of works, so that no one may boast" (Eph. 2:8–9).

Third, *grace* can be used to speak about the support, help, and guidance we receive as a benefit of our salvation. Through the ministry of the Holy Spirit we receive grace and are reborn spiritually, empowered to do good works, and protected from evil and temptation. It is grace in this sense that the Lord speaks of when he tells Paul that "my grace is sufficient for you" (2 Cor. 12:9).

That first way of thinking about grace has to do with who Jesus is. Owen calls this *personal grace*. The second and third ways of thinking about grace have to do with what Jesus accomplished for us by his death and resurrection. Owen calls these *purchased grace* because they are things that Jesus bought for us at the cross. This is very similar to the distinction theologians make between *the person* of Christ (who he is) and *the work* of Christ (what he did for us). Both of those are very important for our relationship to him—we need the grace of who Jesus is and the grace that comes to us because of all that he did for us.

Owen begins by helping us to take a long look at Jesus's personal grace. Here we aren't talking about a grace-filled personal appearance; there is nothing in the Bible that would make us think that Jesus was particularly good-looking or presented himself in a physically impressive way (in fact, see Isaiah 53:2). But when we are talking about Jesus as our mediator, the one sent by the Father to bring us home to him, "in this respect the Scripture describes him [Jesus] as exceedingly excellent, comely [attractive], and desirable—far above comparison with the *chief*, choicest created good, or any endearment imaginable."[1] In short, when you really look at who Jesus is, you will see that he's the best of the best.

1   John Owen, *Communion with the Triune God*, ed. Kelly M. Kapic and Justin Taylor (Wheaton, IL: Crossway, 2007), 145.

Though there is a lot more that could be said, Owen limits himself to talking about three ways that we can see the grace of who Jesus is:

1. He is perfectly suited to save us. No one else and no other kind of person could bring us to God.
2. He is full of grace. We will never find the end of his tenderness and compassion toward us.
3. He is the perfect answer to all our problems. There is no real need you could ever have that doesn't find its solution in Jesus.

Let's start with the first idea, that Jesus is perfectly suited to save us. Jesus is the Son of God who took on human flesh. It might be difficult for us to imagine, but it's worth the effort—Jesus perfectly brings together in one person the natures of God and man. Owen sees Jesus laying one hand on God and one hand on us so that "he fills up all the distance that was made by sin between God and us."[2] If Jesus were not fully God, he would not have "had room enough in his breast to receive, and power enough in his spirit to bear, all the wrath that was prepared for us."[3] If he were not fully man, he would not be able to stand in our place as our substitute. No one could possibly save us from our sins and bring us to God other than one who unites the divine and human nature in person. Jesus is that person, and so he alone is able to save us.

Second, Jesus is full of grace. The bank of his patience, love, compassion, and kindness toward us never runs out. He never

2   Owen, *Communion*, 148.
3   Owen, *Communion*, 148.

reaches the end of his grace, because he has received "the Spirit without measure" (John 3:34), and in him "all the fullness of God" dwells (Col. 1:19). It is out of this overflowing storehouse that he supplies everything we could ever need, so John writes about Jesus that "from his fullness we have all received, grace upon grace" (John 1:16). This is exactly the good news we need to hear right now, because if Jesus's grace had a limit, you and I would have reached it a long time ago! If he only had a limited reserve of kindness toward us, our sin surely would have found its bottom. Jesus is lovely because he is full of grace.

Finally, Jesus is the perfect answer to all our problems. If there's anything you lack when it comes to the things of God, Jesus is what you need. If you are spiritually dead, Jesus is your life (Col. 3:4). If you are weak, Christ is the power of God (1 Cor. 1:24). If you are feeling weighed down by your guilt, Jesus is your holiness and your righteousness (1 Cor. 1:30). Whatever you need, "whether it be life or light, power or joy, all is wrapped up in him."[4]

This is the Son of God, and we get to be his friends! If people really knew him and how amazing he is, everyone would love him. Only those blinded by the devil can fail to see his glory and goodness (1 Cor. 2:8; 2 Cor. 4:4). If you could find something better than Jesus, then you should go ahead and pursue whatever it is with all your might. But you'll never find anything that compares to the grace of Jesus's person.

So ask yourself whether Jesus has the place in your heart that he deserves. If there are other things you delight in more, just ask yourself what they have done for you. What peace have they

4 Owen, *Communion*, 149.

given you? What benefit has anything else been to you when you compare it to the grace and everlasting life that Christ alone gives?

If you find your love for Jesus at a low point right now, all is not lost. You can be certain that his love for you hasn't changed in the slightest, and there is plenty of grace to be found in him. Right now, take time to study him a little. Spend a few moments thinking about the grace of Jesus's person, and let your heart be moved toward him in love.

7

The Perfect Husband

IN THE LAST CHAPTER we began thinking about how we carry out a relationship with God the Son. And while Owen argues that we live out our friendship with the Father with his love at the center, when it comes to the Son, it's all about his grace. That isn't something that Owen came up with on his own; we often see the grace of Jesus highlighted in Scripture as a particular gift to be experienced on a regular basis by his people (e.g., Rom. 16:20; Gal. 6:18; 1 Thess. 5:28; 2 Thess. 3:18). As believers we have communion with Jesus when we delight in the grace of his person (who he is) and when we live in light of the grace he has purchased for us (what he has done to save us and make us his own).

Owen continues his meditation on that first aspect of Jesus's grace—the grace of his person—by unpacking the Bible's use of marriage imagery to describe the way Jesus and his people relate to one another. The New Testament speaks of Jesus as a groom and his people, the church, as a bride (2 Cor. 11:2; Eph. 5:25–27).

You don't have to work too hard to get the sense of what that word picture is meant to describe—marriage is supposed to be the most intimate and personal of all our relationships. Owen describes the way Jesus and his bride (that is, us!) relate to one another by saying, "There is a *mutual resignation*, or making over of their persons one to another. . . . Christ makes himself over to the soul, to be his, as to all the love, care, and tenderness of a husband; and the soul gives up itself wholly unto the Lord Christ, to be his, as to all loving, tender obedience."[1]

We would never dare to think about Jesus this way if the Bible didn't tell us that we should. It is hard to imagine that Jesus would love us this much, that he would give himself to us in the way that a perfectly loving husband would give himself to his wife. But just because it's hard to imagine doesn't mean that it isn't true. Jesus is a husband to us. That means that our communion with the Son of God begins with him moving toward us in tender care and personal affection. He looks at us like a smitten man looks at the woman of his dreams.

Now, if a friendship (or marriage, in this case) is a two-way street, then what is expected of us? You can see why that is an important question. Jesus is always a perfect husband to us; his love and care never fail or diminish. That means that if we are not enjoying a happy relationship with him, we can be sure that the problem is on our end. But what are we to be looking for in our response to him?

Owen lays out two ways that Jesus's people should respond to his love: "the *liking of Christ*, for his *excellency*" and the "*accept-*

1 John Owen, *Communion with the Triune God*, ed. Kelly M. Kapic and Justin Taylor (Wheaton, IL: Crossway, 2007), 155.

ing of Christ by the *will*, as its only husband."[2] As we commune with him, we learn to see Jesus in all his beauty, and we begin to increasingly prefer Jesus over every other thing in the world. We turn our backs on everything that competes with Jesus for our affection, things like the promises of sin, the pleasures of the world, and the allure of self-salvation through religion and hard work.

If carrying on a friendship with Jesus means preferring him above everything else, then one of the most important things we can do is grow in our appreciation for how wonderful he is. In order to do that, it might help us a little if we spend time thinking about just how terrible sin is, how unsatisfying the world's pleasures are in the end, and how our efforts to earn God's love wind up making us miserable. But what our souls need to hear most is not how bad those things are but rather how amazing Jesus is. When we see the beauty of Christ clearly, the pleasures of sin begin to look cheap and fake. The more we feast on his love, the less appetite we have for the things of the world.

To help stir up in us greater love for Jesus, the kind of love that a wife would have for her husband if she was married to the most amazing man who ever lived, Owen gives us a list of just some of the places where we can see something of how lovely Jesus is.

He is lovely in his person. Jesus is the God-man, completely glorious, holy, pure, and full of majesty.

He is lovely in his birth and incarnation. Jesus was rich beyond anything we could imagine, but for our sakes he made himself

---

2 Owen, *Communion*, 157, 158.

poor (2 Cor. 8:9). He stooped so far down to become one of us so that he could save us.

He is lovely in the way that he lived. Jesus always did the right thing, no matter how difficult the circumstances. He lived in poverty and suffered great persecution but only ever did good to others. He never reviled, cursed, or responded to evil with evil.

He is lovely in his death. On the cross, Jesus "carried all our sins into a land of forgetfulness."[3] This is where Jesus is most lovely to sinners. Through his death he has made his bride radiant and spotless (Eph. 5:27).

He is lovely in all that he has done to save us. Jesus is not just lovely in his incarnation and his death but in everything he has done—his resurrection, his ascension into heaven, and his intercession on our behalf (Heb. 7:25–26).

He is lovely in his glory. Jesus is no longer a poor, persecuted sufferer. He has been raised from the dead in glory, seated at the right hand of the Father, and crowned with majesty. He is a terrifying sight to his enemies but still "full of mercy, love, and compassion, toward his beloved ones."[4]

He is lovely in his grace. Jesus, through his Holy Spirit, supplies his people with the grace and comfort they need in their daily lives.

3 Owen, *Communion*, 181.
4 Owen, *Communion*, 181.

He is lovely in his tender care. Jesus protects his people and keeps them spiritually safe in every kind of persecution and opposition.

He is lovely in the worship that he has appointed for us. Jesus hasn't left us to figure out how to draw near, but he has given us ways to worship him and commune with him. We have received baptism, the Lord's Supper, the gift of the Bible, and an invitation to come to him in prayer.

He is lovely in his vengeance. Like a protective husband, Jesus will pour out justice and punishment on everyone who stubbornly opposes him and his bride.

He is lovely in all the gifts he showers on his bride. Jesus gives pardon from sin, a restored relationship with God, peace, joy, comfort, and the sure hope of eternity with him in a world made new (to name just a few!).

This list is meant to be just an appetizer for your spiritual hunger; we could keep going forever, for "there is no end of his excellencies and desirableness."[5] You can be sure that the more you look at Jesus, letting your soul delight in his character and power and kindness, the more lovely he will seem to you. There is only good news when you consider Jesus, for what you see is that the most wonderful person loves you like a husband loves a wife. As great as your sin may be, it is swallowed up by the greatness of your husband's love. He has committed himself to you, and he has sworn to be yours forever.

5   Owen, *Communion*, 182.

This is love that demands a response. After all, there would be something seriously wrong with a wife who wouldn't love being married to the best man in the world. This makes our duty a delight, for we get to love Jesus, the one who has loved us so wonderfully. "Let believers exercise their hearts abundantly unto this thing. This is choice communion with the Son Jesus Christ."[6]

It might be hard for you to imagine, but it actually makes Jesus happy when you love him and delight in him. But it only makes sense, for what husband doesn't enjoy his wife's love? Commit yourself to learning more about him and appreciating his goodness more so that you can grow in your love for him. Make that your goal every time you read the Bible or hear a sermon or sing a hymn or pray or take the Lord's Supper. Allow your mind to ponder all the qualities of Jesus, and increasingly turn away from anything in this world that might compete for your love. Don't delay, but when you finish this little chapter, take time to please Jesus by telling him how much you love him. "Let him know it from us; he delights to hear it."[7]

6 Owen, *Communion*, 158.
7 Owen, *Communion*, 158.

8

The Knowledge of Jesus

WE KNOW THAT FRIENDSHIP requires two people who love and enjoy each other. We also know that Jesus's love for his people is perfect and limitless. After all, if he went to the cross for you, you can be sure that he'll never stop loving you! That means, as I noted in the last chapter, the problem is always on our side. If you aren't enjoying the kind of intimacy and communion with Jesus that the Bible talks about, it's not because Jesus isn't delighting in you; it's because you aren't delighting in him.

The goal here is not to make you feel guilty and condemned, but rather to help you identify ways you can grow in your friendship with Jesus. To help endear Jesus to us more and more, Owen gives us yet another meditation on his excellence and value. This time, we are going to see that Jesus is the only way for us truly to know God and ourselves. He is the only *true* source of two of the most important things in the world—wisdom and knowledge. In this chapter, we will look at two ways that we find wisdom and knowledge in Jesus alone. I hope it helps you see more clearly how wonderful Jesus is.

First, in Jesus we learn what God is like—*we have knowledge of God.* There are some things we can know about God just by looking at the world he has created and the way he rules over it. For example, we can see what God has made and conclude that he is powerful and beautiful and patient with rebellious humanity (see Rom. 1:19–21). But there are some very wonderful things that we can learn about God only when we catch sight of them in the Lord Jesus, particularly that *God loves sinners.*

When the Bible says that "God is love" (1 John 4:8), it means not only that he is loving and tender in his nature, but also that he has always acted in a loving way toward his people. We might expect God to love us if we were righteous and holy, but only through the gift of the Lord Jesus can we really know for certain that he loves us despite our sin. Consider carefully what his word says:

> In this the love of God was made manifest among us, that God sent his only Son into the world, so that we might live through him. In this is love, not that we have loved God but that he loved us and sent his Son to be the propitiation for our sins. (1 John 4:9–10)

> God so loved the world, that he gave his only Son, that whoever believes in him should not perish but have eternal life. (John 3:16)

> God shows his love for us in that while we were still sinners, Christ died for us. (Rom. 5:8)

When you put those passages together, it's clear that Jesus is the ultimate way that God shows his love for the sinful world and for sinful people like you and me. When you want to know whether God loves sinners, simply look to God's gift of his Son for your answer.

It's also the case that we know about *God's pardoning mercy* only because of Christ. You can look at a mountain or a flower or the moon all day, but you'll never conclude from those things that God is willing to forgive and graciously accept sinners. For that, you need to look to Jesus as well, for "it is wholly treasured up in him and revealed by him. . . . Had not God set forth the Lord Christ, all the angels in heaven and men on earth could not have apprehended that there had been any such thing in the nature of God as this grace of pardoning mercy."[1]

The great question that hung over the Old Testament was this: How can God be merciful? We should be able to easily understand that he is just and will not leave sin unpunished (Ex. 34:7). But how can he *also* be a God who is, as he told Moses, "merciful and gracious, slow to anger, and abounding in steadfast love and faithfulness, keeping steadfast love for thousands, forgiving iniquity and transgression and sin" (Ex. 34:6–7)?

You see the tension: how can a just God *also* be a God of pardoning mercy? Either he is going to take sin seriously or he is going to mercifully pardon it, but it seems impossible for him to do both. That's where Jesus comes in and resolves for us the great tension of the ages, for in him God's justice and pardoning mercy meet and finally make sense. Because Jesus bore the punishment

1 John Owen, *Communion with the Triune God*, ed. Kelly M. Kapic and Justin Taylor (Wheaton, IL: Crossway, 2007), 187–88.

and wrath that our sins deserve, God's perfect justice is satisfied. And since our sins have been paid for at the cross of Christ, God can freely pardon sinners without being in any way unjust (see Rom. 3:21–26).

If it weren't for Jesus, anything we might know about God would ultimately be bad news for us. God's justice would be terrifying; his mercy would seem hopelessly far away. But in Jesus, God has made his glory something we can see and understand. Because the Father sent the Son to die for us, all the qualities and characteristics of God that might terrify us have been put to use doing good to our souls for all eternity. As Owen puts it, "These attributes of God, so manifested and exercised, are *powerful and able* to bring us to the everlasting fruition of him."[2]

This knowledge of God is a wonderful gift. We aren't left to guess what he is like or to worship a god that is nothing more than a reflection of our own preferences and wishes. Instead, Jesus shows us a picture of a God who is far better—more holy, more loving, more kind toward us—than we could ever imagine.

The second way that Jesus gives us wisdom and knowledge is that he shows us what we are like—*we have knowledge of ourselves.* Only when we look to him do we really understand who we are and what we are like. Specifically, the work of Jesus on the cross shows us what it means that we are sinners. We might be tempted to take our sin lightly, to excuse it by pleading good intentions or even blame our environment and upbringing. But when we see the infinitely beautiful and holy Son of God suffering under the wrath that we deserve, hanging in the darkness, forsaken by his

2 Owen, *Communion*, 199.

Father, we can't play games any longer. When we look to Christ on the cross, we can begin to understand something of what our sin deserves. When we see who it was that had to die for us, we can be sure that we had no hope of ever saving ourselves.

But that's not the end of the story, because Jesus also shows us that sin is no longer the core of who we are, for in him we are now righteous. Because we are united to him and he made an end of sin through his death and resurrection, we are dead to sin as well (Rom. 6:9–11). But Jesus hasn't just taken away our sin by his death; that actually wouldn't be enough for us to be saved. It's not enough for us to be cleansed from our sin and declared innocent; we need to be *made righteous* so we can stand before God.

Jesus provides that righteousness for us. He is able to save us because he lived a life of perfect obedience to his Father, fulfilling God's law and keeping his commandments. As a result of his obedience, he has righteousness that can be counted to us when we are united to him by faith (Phil. 3:9).

We live in a world that encourages us to take our identity from any number of things. We are told that the most important thing we can do is look inside ourselves to discover our identity, our worth, and our value. But God's word puts a finger under our chin and raises our gaze up so that we can look at Jesus. He is the one who shows us who we truly are—sinners who have been declared righteous by the life and death of our Savior—and frees us to live our lives in light of that identity.

Jesus shows us what God is like and what we are like. Without him it would be impossible to have any kind of friendship with God, for we were lost in darkness and far off and fearful of his holiness. But God demonstrates his great love and pardoning mercy through the gift of his Son, and in him we are given the righteousness we need in order to approach God with the boldness and confidence of a friend.

Remember that the goal of all of this is to "draw our hearts to the more cheerful entertainment of and delight in the Lord Jesus."[3] When you look at Jesus, you see truth that you would never find in the finest university. He provides us with knowledge of God and ourselves that cannot be found in the best book of philosophy, in the most powerful poem, or in the most profound novel. In Jesus are hidden all riches of knowledge (Col. 2:3), so anyone who wants to be wise will want to be his friend!

3   Owen, *Communion*, 228.

9

A True Friend's Delight

IN ORDER TO EXPERIENCE fully our friendship with the Lord Jesus, we must believe that he delights in us. That makes sense, because people don't look forward to spending time with someone who merely tolerates them, or worse, dislikes them. Think about the people in your life whom you are most excited to be around. My guess is that you feel that they enjoy your company as much as you do theirs. It's a wonderful feeling to see joy in someone else's eyes, be it a friend, a child, a spouse, a parent, or a grandparent, just because you've arrived. We never mature too far beyond the wobbly insecurities of our adolescence. We like to be liked.

Now, we know that Jesus loves his people; who could look at him bleeding on the cross for us and doubt his love? But that's not exactly the same thing as saying that he *likes* us. I can love someone and not enjoy him all that much. There are people in my life whom I love and for whose well-being I would gladly sacrifice whatever is necessary, but (if I'm being perfectly honest) I really don't like them very much or enjoy spending time with them. Their personalities grate on me; they do things that irritate me, and it's likely that they feel the same way about me. We love each other, but we're not friends. Love and delight are different things. So we know that Jesus loves his people, but can we say that he also delights in us, that he enjoys us and wants to have us around? You can see why that is a crucial question for our relationship with him.

Well, the answer is a resounding yes! Owen argues that "Christ delights exceedingly in his saints" by yet again pressing the significance of the wedding imagery in the Bible (see Song 3:11; Isa. 62:5).[1] Speaking of our normal experience of weddings he writes:

> It is known that usually this is the most *unmixed* delight that the sons of men are in their pilgrimage made partakers of. The delight of a bridegroom in the days of his espousals [wedding] is the height of what an expression of delight can be carried unto. This is in Christ answerable to the relation he takes us into. His heart is glad in us, without sorrow. And every day while we live is his *wedding day*. . . . The thoughts of communion with the saints were the joy of his heart from eternity.[2]

Because of our sin and the weakness of our faith, it can be hard for us to believe that Jesus really feels this way about us. As a result, we may find ourselves keeping our emotional distance from him, fearing that if we come to him, we will experience not delight but disapproval. In order to help convince us, Owen offers

1 John Owen, *Communion with the Triune God*, ed. Kelly M. Kapic and Justin Taylor (Wheaton, IL: Crossway, 2007), 229.
2 Owen, *Communion*, 230.

us one proof (out of many) of Christ's delight: he has told us his thoughts and enables us to tell him ours.

You can see how that's a sign that Jesus really does view us with joy and love, right? I don't share my deepest thoughts with strangers. You don't tell your most intimate secrets to someone you don't like very much. But Jesus shares his heart and mind with the people in whom he delights. He wants us to know him, and he wants us to feel that he knows us. That's why he sent his Spirit, so that through his word we might have the "mind of Christ" (1 Cor. 2:10–16). Speaking of Jesus, Owen writes:

> He, then, communicates his mind unto his saints, and *them only*—his mind, the counsel of his love, the thoughts of his heart, the purposes of his bosom, for our eternal good. . . . There is not anything in the heart of Christ, wherein these his friends are concerned, that he does not reveal to them. All his *love*, his *goodwill*, the *secrets* of his covenant, the *paths* of obedience, the *mystery* of faith, is told them.[3]

A lot of people think that there is no way to really know God. To them, it seems proud and arrogant to think that human beings have access to truth about the great mysteries of the universe—who we are, who made us, why we are here. It seems that the most humble and honest thing to do is throw our hands up in the air and admit that we don't really know anything. And that would be true, *if* Jesus didn't care about us and hadn't revealed himself to us. The fact is, Jesus hasn't left us in the dark to guess what he

3 Owen, *Communion*, 231–32.

is like and how we should feel about him, so the most humble thing we can do is take him at his word. He told his disciples, "No longer do I call you servants, for the servant does not know what his master is doing; but I have called you friends, for all that I have heard from my Father I have made known to you" (John 15:15). Jesus has revealed to us his glory and power (Mark 9:2–8), his gentleness and mercy (Matt. 11:28–30), and even his plans for world history (Rev. 1:17–19). He shows that he wants us for his friends by revealing what is important to him.

But that's not all. Jesus doesn't just reveal his thoughts to us; he also makes it possible for us to reveal ourselves to him. It's not enough to know what Jesus is thinking and doing; he wants us to communicate the deepest thoughts and feelings of our souls. Now, it is true that Jesus already knows those things about me; in fact, he knows them better than I do. But that fact alone doesn't offer much comfort or make me feel like I have a close relationship with him. After all, the government knows a lot about me, but I don't consider it my friend. In order to have a sense of communion with Jesus, I need to share my heart with him.

Just yesterday, I had lunch with one of my closest friends, someone I have known for a long time. I had been going through a difficult personal situation, and it was such a gift to be able to talk about it with someone who loves me and cares. As I shared with my friend, I talked through the ways that I was feeling tempted toward fear and regret in light of the situation. He asked questions and offered some encouragement and advice, and we prayed together. And although my situation didn't change at all over the course of our lunch, it made a real difference to be able to tell a friend about what was going on.

Friendships like that are a gift from God, and they are meant to point us beyond themselves to an even greater friend, Jesus himself. Whatever solace you might take from sharing your life with someone else, it is nothing compared to the joy and comfort that comes when you share your heart with Jesus. There is no such thing as *oversharing* with Jesus. When it comes to him, you will never have to worry that you'll veer into TMI (too much information) territory, where you find yourself having shared more information about yourself than the relationship warrants. Because he delights in you, *Jesus wants you to bring him the deepest things that are in your heart.* Because he wants to be your friend, he has done everything necessary for you to share your deepest, truest self with him.

The good news is that you don't even have to be very good at this kind of thing. Maybe you aren't used to acknowledging what is really going on in your heart. Perhaps you are afraid of the stew of fear, sadness, and shame you will find in there if you take the lid off. Or, if you are like me, you might sometimes feel that you do not know how to put what you're feeling into words. But Jesus knows our weakness, and he has it taken care of.

If you don't know what to say or even what is going on in your heart, Jesus has given you his Spirit to help you (Rom. 8:26–27). If you feel like you aren't worthy to come before him, Jesus gives you boldness by the cleansing power of his blood (Heb. 10:20). If you are worried that Jesus doesn't really care, his pierced hands tell you everything you need to know. He died so that you can be his friend.

The best way to experience this kind of communion with God the Son is simply to pray to him now. You don't have to wait until your thoughts are organized and sanitized, for he is a friend who is always glad to hear from you. Just go to him and share your thoughts, your fears, your temptations, your needs, and your deepest desires. He has told you how he feels about you, and he wants you to share your heart with him.

10

Treasured

JESUS TREASURES YOU. Let that sink in for a second. Ordinary, sinful, limited old *you* are of infinite value to the precious, mighty, glorious Son of God. That is the only way to explain his desire for communion with you. If he didn't value you highly, he wouldn't have gone to such great lengths to make you his friend. For that reason, Owen continues his consideration of our communion with God the Son by seeking to demonstrate just how highly he values believers and how we ought to respond to that kind of love. Let me share with you three things to which Owen directs our attention.

First, speaking of Jesus's love for believers he writes, "*All that ever he did or does, all that he underwent or suffered . . . was for their sakes.*"[1]

- For our sake Jesus took on human flesh and human nature, with all its limitation, frailty, and weakness. He left the

1   John Owen, *Communion with the Triune God*, ed. Kelly M. Kapic and Justin Taylor (Wheaton, IL: Crossway, 2007), 247.

glories of heaven to be born in obscurity and poverty. He didn't cling tightly to the honor and glory that he deserved as the Son of God, but rather he took on the form of a servant and was willing to be treated as nothing (Phil. 2:5–7).

- For our sake Jesus endured the cross. He was betrayed by someone close to him, denied by his friend Peter, and mocked by gloating enemies. He experienced incredible physical pain as he was beaten, nailed to a cross, and lifted up to die. And worst of all, on the cross he bore the curse that we deserve for our sins. There he was forsaken by his heavenly Father and experienced the wrath of God that we deserve because of our rebellion.

- For our sake Jesus rose from the dead and is seated in heaven, where he intercedes on our behalf before the Father (Heb. 7:23–25).

All of that was and is for you. If you look at what Jesus was willing to give up and what he was willing to endure and what he does now for the sake of his people, you can only conclude that he must place the highest value on them. Owen summarizes it in this way: "He parted with the greatest glory, he underwent the greatest misery, he does the greatest works there ever were, because he loves his spouse—because he values believers."[2]

The second proof of just how highly Jesus values his people is the fact that he protects them for all eternity. Even if every power

2 Owen, *Communion*, 254.

in the universe combined to try to take his sheep out of his hand, he will never lose even one. He prayed to the Father to keep them (John 17:11) and commits us to his care so that not one of his people can be snatched out of his hand. We see the depth of his love in the fact that Jesus took away the one thing that could threaten to undo us eternally and ruin us spiritually—our sin. Imagine that. In his holiness Jesus's soul hates sin more than sinful people like you and me could ever imagine. But in his great love for his people, instead of losing us to our sin, "he hides all, covers all, bears with all, rather than he will lose them. . . . Oh, the world of sinful follies that our dear Lord Jesus bears with on this account!"[3]

The third proof of the value that Jesus places on his people is the pity and compassion with which he looks on us. Because he took on our flesh and our nature when he became a man, and because he bore our sin at the cross, Jesus always understands what we are going through. It's just different when you have that sort of friend. If I'm going through a difficult time with one of my kids, I can get help and sympathy from a friend who doesn't have children. But it's even better to talk with a friend who has experienced the same kind of struggle; he will be able to offer a more personal compassion.

In the same way, Jesus is able to help us in our times of temptation, for he himself experienced intense temptation and satanic opposition (Luke 4:1–13). He knows what it is like to be mistreated and misunderstood, so he is perfectly sympathetic toward us in our misery. As a result, we can always be sure that he is a source of grace and mercy to us in our times of need (Heb. 4:15–16).

3   Owen, *Communion*, 255.

Jesus places such a high value on us that he came and died and rose and lives for us. He pours out his love and mercy and compassion and help and grace on his people, not sparingly or meagerly but plentifully. "Whatever he gives us—his grace to assist us, his presence to comfort us—he does it abundantly. . . . Christ deals bountifully with us."[4]

In response to such love, believers strive to be faithful to him and to value him more than anything else. We receive his perfect, abundant love for us and respond with our (sometimes weak and poor) love for him. We see all that Jesus did and does for us, and we are moved to treasure him more than any other thing or person. Believers come to value Jesus more than their own lives (John 12:24–26), more than their families (Luke 14:26), more than success and fame and the approval of the world (Phil. 3:7–8).

It bears repeating that if there is anything lacking in our communion with Jesus, we can be sure that the problem is on our end. Since Jesus's care for us is abundant and overflowing, anything missing from our friendship is our responsibility. Owen puts it this way: "If in any things, then, we are straitened [restricted], it is in ourselves; Christ deals bountifully with us. Indeed, the great sin of believers is that they make not use of Christ's bounty as they ought to do; that we do not every day take of him mercy in abundance."[5] We have all the resources we will ever need in our spiritual lives; we need only look to him when we need help.

One practical way that you can treasure Jesus in your life and cultivate your communion with him is by pursuing holiness and obedience to his commands. We might be tempted to feel that

4 Owen, *Communion*, 268–69.
5 Owen, *Communion*, 269.

obedience to Jesus is somehow on the opposite side of the street from a friendship with Jesus. Maybe you've even heard people say something to the effect that being a Christian "isn't rules, but a relationship." And as far as it goes, that is true; we don't earn God's favor simply by performing rituals and trying to keep his law as best we can.

But if you understand the gospel, and the good news that God is transforming us into the image of his Son, and that all his commands lead us to what is good and right and pleasing to him, then how could friendship with Jesus look like anything but obedience? If our sin and his commitment to destroy it sent the Lord to the cross, how can we claim to love him without wanting to put sin away from us? The Lord makes this connection for us in John's Gospel: "You are my friends *if you do what I command you*" (John 15:14).

To be clear, our obedience is only ever acceptable and pleasing to God because of Jesus's work on our behalf. All our duties are "weak, imperfect, and not able to abide in the presence of God,"[6] but Jesus cleans them up and bears them before the Father for us. We must recognize that when we do what Jesus tells us to do, when we avoid sin and pursue love and holiness, we are taking an important step toward living out our friendship with him. Owen says of the obedience of believers, "They have a special regard to their dear Lord Jesus. He is, on all these accounts, and innumerable others, continually in their thoughts."[7]

If you have ever had a season in your life where you slipped into disobedience and sin, my guess is that you felt a disruption in

6 Owen, *Communion*, 270.
7 Owen, *Communion*, 270.

your communion with Jesus. You simply won't enjoy his presence if you're mistreating your spouse or consuming pornography or stealing money from your workplace. You won't feel Jesus's closeness and pleasure if you are withholding love from your brothers and sisters in the church, failing to be generous to those in need, or refusing to forgive those who sin against you.

Jesus treasures you. He has shown that to be true in word and deed, in the past, present, and future. The great work of your life is to treasure him in return by "the contemplation of the excellencies, desirableness, love, and grace of our dear Lord Jesus."[8] If you have not been walking in happy obedience to his commands, you don't have to stay away. You don't need to worry whether Jesus will receive you when you go to him. Jesus has always cherished you, despite your sin. Don't waste another day on sin. Respond to his friendship and love with joyful obedience.

8 Owen, *Communion*, 270.

11

Costly Grace

JOHN OWEN'S main argument regarding our relationship with God the Son is that it is carried out according to his grace. Back in chapter 6 we thought briefly about the distinction that Owen made between the *personal grace* of Jesus and his *purchased grace*, between the grace that comes to us because of who Jesus is and the grace we experience because of what he has done for us in his death, resurrection, and ascension into heaven. To this point, we have been considering the personal grace of Jesus, particularly in the way that he loves us, values us, and serves to reveal God to us. Now we turn our attention to look more directly at the purchased grace of Christ and particularly how our friendship with him springs up from three aspects of his ministry to us—his life, his death, and his intercession.

First, Jesus purchased grace for us by the obedience of his earthly life. It might be tempting to think that Jesus began his work of saving us at his crucifixion, but the truth is that the way he lived his entire life was essential to our salvation. Otherwise he could have simply died a much younger man. But there is a reason that Jesus didn't offer up his life until the time was right (John 12:23), until he had done everything that was required of him so that he would be qualified to act as our Savior.

Jesus was always nothing but obedient to the will of his heavenly Father; he never thought, felt, said, or did anything contrary to the will of God. He was perfectly holy (Heb. 7:26) and always kept in step with the mind of God. He never looked at a woman lustfully, he was never sinfully angry, and he never lied. But even more than that, he also kept the instructions and commands of God's law perfectly. He self-consciously came "to fulfill all righteousness" (Matt. 3:15), so he proactively did all the things God required from his people in his word. Jesus was circumcised when he was an infant according to God's command; he obeyed his parents, kept the Sabbath, and loved the Lord with all his heart.

Jesus's obedience purchased grace for us, for we needed more than just the forgiveness that came through his death. His death was sufficient to wipe away our sin and declare us innocent before God, but we need more than that—we need to be made righteous in order to have hope of eternity in the presence of God. To illustrate the idea, imagine that you have been invited to a feast in the presence of a great king. But there's a problem. Your only set of clothes is filthy and disgusting beyond repair. In that case, you need two things: a way to get rid of your filthy clothes and a clean set that you can wear to the feast. In this picture, your sin is that filthy set of clothing, and it is the death of Jesus that removes it from you. Because of his obedience, he has a righteousness that becomes ours when we come to him in faith. He is able to clothe his people in the holiness of his perfect obedience (Zech. 3:1–5; Matt. 22:11–13).

The second way that Jesus purchased grace for us was his death on the cross. Owen doesn't dwell for long on this topic, mostly because he writes so much about it in other places. But we should make no mistake: "The death of Christ . . . is a principle spring and fountain of that grace wherein we have communion with him."[1] On the cross Jesus paid the price required to deliver us from the wrath and curse that we have earned for ourselves. It was a price paid to God, who stood against us as our holy judge and to whom we owed an insurmountable debt (Matt. 18:22–23). In his death, Jesus offered himself as a sacrifice in our place and took all the punishment that we deserve. By his death, Jesus removed everything that would keep us from being God's friend.

The third way that Jesus purchased grace for us was by rising from the dead and interceding before his heavenly Father on our behalf. If he had stayed in the grave, his saving work would have remained there with him, but he rose and entered heaven "to appear in the presence of God on our behalf" (Heb. 9:24). Think of Jesus as your defense attorney, representing your interests in the court of heaven, pointing to his own blood as proof of your innocence, and praying for all your needs before your loving heavenly Father. This is what the author of Hebrews means when he writes, speaking of Jesus, "Consequently, he is able to save to the uttermost those who draw near to God through him, since he always lives to make intercession for them" (Heb. 7:25). Jesus

---

1   John Owen, *Communion with the Triune God*, ed. Kelly M. Kapic and Justin Taylor (Wheaton, IL: Crossway, 2007), 287.

is alive right now and is preserving your salvation at this very moment.

As a result, you never have to fear being disqualified from God's love because of your sin. There will never be a moment that Jesus isn't on your side, in heaven as an ever-living reminder that the price has been paid for you to be brought into the family of God. Even when you are asleep, he is wide awake and on your side in heaven. As Paul writes, "Who is to condemn? Christ Jesus is the one who died—more than that, who was raised—who is at the right hand of God, who indeed is interceding for us" (Rom. 8:34).

So those are the sources of the grace that Jesus has purchased for us—his perfect life of obedience to God, his death on the cross, and his ongoing ministry of intercession. And while it is wonderful that Jesus did all those things, for our purposes we need to ask how those things apply to us and our friendship with him. The answer is found in the union we have with Jesus in all that he did.

When you became a follower of Christ, the Holy Spirit united you spiritually to Jesus. Now, spiritually speaking, it is as if you have done the things that he did, and you have experienced the things that happened to him. This explains some of what the apostle Paul wrote in his letters to the ancient churches:

We were buried therefore with him. (Rom. 6:4)

I have been crucified with Christ. (Gal. 2:20)

[God the Father] made us alive together with Christ . . . and raised us up with him and seated us with him in the heavenly places in Christ Jesus. (Eph. 2:5–6)

Having been buried with him . . . (Col. 2:12)

And you . . . God made alive together with him. (Col. 2:13)

You have been raised with Christ. (Col. 3:1)

If we have died with him . . . (2 Tim. 2:11)

These spiritual realities form the foundation for our friendship with the Son of God. If you are one of Jesus's people by faith, then every one of these things is true of you, whether you feel like it or not on any given day. The pressures and problems of everyday life might seem like a massive mountain blocking your vision and making your enjoyment of your relationship with Jesus feel like a luxury that you simply cannot afford. But the truth is that your life—your identity, the most important thing about you—doesn't primarily belong here on earth.

Instead, "you have died, and your life is hidden with Christ" (Col. 3:3). The old you, the one who belonged here in this world of sin and sorrow, died with Christ. There is a new you who was raised along with him and seated with him in heaven. This is so significant to who you are that Paul can say that Christ "is your life" (Col. 3:4).

This means that communion with Jesus isn't something weird, strange, or unnatural. It is simply a matter of being who you are, living your daily life with an ever-increasing awareness of your true identity and the purpose of your salvation. This will involve some effort on your part, and most of that effort will begin in your mind with the way you think about things. Remember that

Paul tells the church, "Set your minds on things that are above" (Col. 3:2) and, "Consider yourselves dead to sin and alive to God in Christ Jesus" (Rom. 6:11).

If you are in Christ, you have died and have been raised and are seated with Christ in the heavenly places. All of that is true of you, even if you don't act like it on any given day. But friendship with Jesus is learning to live in light of this purchased grace that has been poured out on you. Sin tempts us to think of our lives only in terms of the limited, momentary pleasures that this world can offer. Suffering sometimes threatens to overwhelm us, and sadness can cloud our vision of Jesus. In those cases, communion with God the Son means locating our ultimate hope in him (1 Pet. 1:13) and understanding our lives in light of all that he has done for us.

12

Cleansing Grace

HAVING SHOWN US how Jesus "purchases" grace for us by his life, death, resurrection, and intercession, Owen moves on in the next chapter of his work to consider the nature of that grace, both what it is like and how we experience it in our relationship with the Lord. We can think about the topic under three headings.

First, there is our acceptance with God, and here Owen is addressing what is often referred to as the believer's *justification*. In our sin, we are not welcomed in his presence but rather are alienated from him, guilty, and condemned (John 3:36; Eph. 2:12–13). It's not pleasant to think about, but it's true. Our selfishness, lust, pride, anger, and rebellion make us morally repulsive to a perfectly holy and loving God. In order to be welcomed by him and to stand in "the presence of his glory with great joy" (Jude 24), we need to have the stink and filth of sin washed off of us. God has a legitimate beef with us, and there's nothing we can do unless someone takes away the cause of the offense.

That's exactly what Jesus has done for us in his death and resurrection. He took the curse of our sin on himself at the cross and paid the price for our freedom and forgiveness. As a result, God has nothing against anyone who is in Christ by faith. Jesus has taken all our shame and guilt on himself, and it is no longer relevant to our situation. The apostle Paul describes it this way: "You, who were dead in your trespasses and the uncircumcision of your flesh, God made alive together with him, having forgiven us all our trespasses, by canceling the record of debt that stood against us with its legal demands. This he set aside, nailing it to the cross" (Col. 2:13–14).

In the courtroom of the universe, there were many "legal demands" that stood against you, the claims of justice that your sin be punished. But all of that has been "set aside," declared no longer relevant to your case, and the guilty verdict against you has been nailed to the cross of Christ. Owen comments on this glorious truth: "What court among men would admit of evidence that has been publicly cancelled and nailed up for all to see it?"[1] Our eternal friendship with Jesus is truly, in the words of an old hymn, a blood-sealed one.

But as we thought about briefly in the last chapter, just cleansing our souls from the stain of our guilt isn't enough to make us acceptable to God. As Owen says about the forgiveness of our sins, "the old quarrel may be laid aside, and yet no new friendship begun; we may be not sinners, and yet not be so far righteous as to have a right to the kingdom of heaven."[2] That friendship and acceptance

---

1   John Owen, *Communion with the Triune God*, ed. Kelly M. Kapic and Justin Taylor (Wheaton, IL: Crossway, 2007), 290.
2   Owen, *Communion*, 290.

by God is begun when the obedience and holiness of Jesus are credited to us. We'll think about this more in the next chapter.

The second heading under which we can think about our experience of the grace of Jesus is our *sanctification*. To sanctify something is to make it holy, and in this instance we are talking about the way that God makes sinners holy by the grace of Jesus. If you are in Christ, you are made holy. Your old sin nature is being transformed into a nature that loves the Lord (Col. 3:9–10), and the guilt you have earned for all the actual sins you've committed has been washed away. Sanctification means not only that we are loved by God but that God makes us to be actually *lovely* in his sight.

Every Christian needs this kind of cleansing, not just once but throughout our whole lives. Even our best deeds are stained by sin on this side of heaven. I can't help but be dogged by self-interest and pride, even when I am trying to serve the Lord with the best of motives. But the grace of Jesus is like a refiner's fire, cleansing out the impurities in our service and preserving only what is valuable. Owen writes, "The saints' good works shall meet them one day with a changed countenance, that they shall scarce know them: that which seemed to them to be black, deformed, defiled, shall appear beautiful and glorious; they shall not be afraid of them, but rejoice to see and follow them."[3] We will think more about this in a future chapter as well.

The third category that describes our experience of Jesus's purchased grace is the privileges we have with and before God. We will leave this for a fuller discussion in a later chapter as well, but

3 Owen, *Communion*, 292.

for now we can think of these privileges in terms of our adoption into God's family and then all the favor and blessings that flow to us as a result of that status. All the good things that come to us from the hand of our heavenly Father—his care, love, kindness, and provision for all our needs—they come to us only because Jesus has purchased them for us by his blood.

Put together, these three categories basically cover all that we will ever receive from Christ in his grace. Our experience of them in this life may be marred by our sin, our weakness, and our lack of understanding. But when we are with Jesus in a world that has been purged of all sickness, sadness, and sin (Rev. 21:3–4), we will finally know the depth and beauty of our salvation fully (1 Cor. 13:12). At that time, we will comprehend just how marvelously we have been loved, saved, and protected by our God (see Paul's prayer in Ephesians 3:14–21). A believer's experience of eternity will be one of acceptance, sanctification, and unimaginable privileges. Speaking of these things Owen comments, "Drive them up to perfection, and you have that which we call everlasting glory. Perfect acceptance, perfect holiness, perfect adoption, or inheritance of sons—that is glory."[4]

Friendship with Jesus in this time and place, then, is a foretaste of what it will be like to be with God forever in a world that has been remade. When we enjoy some sense of his grace along with the acceptance, holiness, and privilege that come with it, we are experiencing a small splinter of what it will be like to be in glory. And one way that we live out this future heavenly reality in our daily lives is by pursuing sanctification and purity here and now.

4 Owen, *Communion*, 293.

If we will live forever in a place of holiness and grace, we ought to strive to live in light of those things now.

Given all we have seen, it will probably come as no surprise that the motivation and power for a life lived in that way cannot come from us. We are pretty much always the problem, and Jesus is the solution. While we are called to work and strive for holiness and growth in godliness (Heb. 12:14), we are always dependent on the work and love of Jesus for the ability to do so. Owen lists for us three ways that the grace of Jesus makes us holy.

1. He sends the Spirit to dwell in us. There is a reason that he is called the *Holy* Spirit—he is holy, and he produces holiness in his people. The Spirit is the one who gives us a new nature and compels us to greater sanctification, and he is poured out on us through Jesus alone (Titus 3:6). The greatest gift that Jesus gives to aid us in our holiness is the gift of the Spirit. As the Spirit lives in us and we learn to follow his guidance, we find ourselves growing in godliness and walking in friendship with the Savior, who sent him to us.

2. Jesus also implants, as it were, a principle of grace in us that counteracts the natural lusts that ruled our lives before we became Christians. "This is the grace that dwells in us, makes its abode with us. . . . In the understanding, it is *light*; in the will, *obedience*; in the affections, *love*; in all, *faith*."[5] This grace in us leads us to delight in him above all others and rest on him in faith.

5 Owen, *Communion*, 293.

3. The grace of Christ also gives us "actual influence" to empower us to do all that we have been commanded to do.[6] Without him, we can do nothing (John 15:5), so we are daily dependent on him for all that we need. He must work in us "to will and to work for his good pleasure" (Phil. 2:13) if we are to grow in obedience and godliness.

This means that communion with Jesus is a matter of regularly going to him, acknowledging your need for help, and asking him to provide all you need so that you can walk in holiness. We can pray that prayer with boldness and confidence, knowing that Jesus died to purchase grace for us. Because he shed his blood for us, we know that sin is no longer central to our identity; we are now accepted and adopted, destined for a life of holiness and blessing. As Jesus's friends, we get a head start on that life in the here and now.

6 Owen, *Communion*, 293.

13

The Drama of Friendship

IN THE LAST CHAPTER, we were introduced to three aspects of Jesus's purchased grace that allow us to have communion with him: acceptance, sanctification, and privileges. Having sketched out these categories for us broadly, Owen moves on in the next three chapters of his work to complete his consideration of friendship with God the Son by taking a deeper dive into each. He begins by returning to the glorious truth we have seen, that the grace of Jesus justifies believers, taking away our guilt and giving us the righteousness we need to be acceptable to God.

But Owen is not primarily concerned to describe justification; his goal is to help us commune more closely with the Lord Jesus. So having described (at some length) the way that the death of Christ cleanses us and the obedience of Christ provides a righteousness for us, Owen proceeds to "show what also is required and performed on our part for the completing thereof."[1] At first

1   John Owen, *Communion with the Triune God*, ed. Kelly M. Kapic and Justin Taylor (Wheaton, IL: Crossway, 2007), 310.

glance, that's a shocking thing for him to write, because it seems to suggest that our acceptance before God is somehow incomplete, that there is something that the believer must do in order to finish Jesus's work. To be clear, that is not what Owen is suggesting. If our acceptance with God depends on our response or obedience in even the slightest way, we have no hope. Rather, Owen is pointing out a glorious truth, one that stands at the heart of his book—God's work of salvation hasn't reached its completion, its final purpose, until it has brought us into an intimate relationship with him. The purchased grace of Jesus does more than make us acceptable to God; its work isn't complete until you and I have responded with faith and love, until we have been brought into communion with him.

The question for us then is this: What does it look like for us to live out this communion with Jesus in our daily life, when we sit down to pray in our living rooms or at our kitchen tables? Well, it begins with something that might surprise us—a deep dive into a sense of our sinfulness. The world we live in teaches us that thinking negative thoughts about ourselves is emotionally unhealthy and that the key to happiness is high self-esteem and self-regard, so it is important for us to see that while the Bible teaches believers to be happy and confident in their standing before God, it takes a very different path to that goal than the one our world recommends. Before we can really experience the peaks of joy that friendship with Jesus brings, we must first take a deep dive into the guilt of our sin.

This is something that we ought to do every day. We must keep in mind the fact that we can never stand before God on the basis of anything good in us. Nothing we have done or will ever do can make us right with him. Remembering this will help us grow in humility and in a sense of dependence on God's mercy. Owen reminds believers that they must also "daily weigh all their *particular actions* in the balance and find them wanting."[2] This involves not only confessing our sinful actions and attitudes—the outbursts of anger, the flare-ups of pride, the unkind words that characterize even the godliest Christian—but also recognizing that even our very best attempts to serve and obey the Lord are tainted by sin. In a sense, it's when I am at my best that I see most clearly how far short I fall of God's righteous standard. When I think of how God sees the vanity and selfishness and pride that cling closely to me when I am trying to serve him, it shields me from the spiritually destructive idea that I can earn his love by my own personal goodness. It also drives me to rejoice in all that Jesus has done for me.

Our goal, however, is not to wallow in negative thoughts about ourselves. Rather, it's to take a deep and honest look into our lives and then bring the weight of our guilt, shame, and failure to Jesus through prayer and meditation. Owen imagines this process as a kind of drama that unfolds in three steps. First, Jesus calls to us in our sin:

> "Come with your burdens; come, you poor soul, with your guilt of sin . . . this is mine," says Christ. "This agreement I made with my Father, that I should come, and take your sins, and bear them away; they were my lot. Give me your *burden*, give me all your *sins*. You know not what to do with them; I know

2 Owen, *Communion*, 311.

how to dispose of them well enough, so that God shall be glorified, and your soul delivered."[3]

What a wonderful friend we have in Jesus, that he would carry away all our grief and sin like this!

God's people respond to these gracious words with humble faith, giving their sins over to Christ. This is the second step in the great drama. Owen describes it this way, speaking of believers:

> They lay down *their sins at the cross of Christ,* upon his shoulders. This is faith's great and bold venture upon the grace, faithfulness, and truth of God, to stand by the cross and say, "Ah! he is bruised for my sins, and wounded for my transgressions, and the chastisement of my peace is upon him. He is thus made sin for me. Here I give up my sins to him that is able to bear them, to undergo them. He requires it of my hands, that I should be content that he should undertake for them; and that I heartily consent unto."[4]

The third and final step in this drama of communion is for the believer to take hold of the righteousness that Jesus offers. In him, we receive everything we need to be accepted in God's presence. Owen calls it the "blessed bartering and exchange of faith,"[5] and as a result, we leave our interaction with Jesus very different from how we were when we entered. The burden of sin is gone, replaced by the beauty of Christ.

3 Owen, *Communion*, 317.
4 Owen, *Communion*, 318.
5 Owen, *Communion*, 318.

To be clear, Owen is not suggesting that we only receive forgiveness for our sins if we intentionally bring them to Jesus. We know that our right standing before God is a one-time gift that need never be repeated. We are speaking here of our communion with Jesus, the daily experience of his love and friendship. And that communion happens when we walk through this little drama in our minds and hearts. It's not too difficult to picture. Imagine that you come into Jesus's presence carrying a heavy, foul-smelling bag filled with your sin and corruption. After you've looked carefully at your soul and your life, you've seen that the picture isn't pretty. And so you are daily weighed down by guilt, rightfully ashamed for all your sinful deeds and attitudes. Maybe you're afraid that Jesus won't be willing to help you, but you hear his gracious call for you to come to him (that's step 1). Convinced that he loves you and is able to help you, you hand that nasty burden over to him (that's step 2). Finally, you take hold of the beautiful gift of his love and holiness that Jesus has purchased for you (that's step 3). In this way, you can go about your day, not crushed by a sense of your sin but confident that God loves you and treasures you.

Can you see how this is so much better than anything the world can offer? This is not some thin, watery nonsense about learning to forgive yourself and cherishing your inner beauty. That is what gets preached to us from movies, magazines, and social-media posts as if it were the discovery of some truly good news. But it is like the makeup they put on a dead body so that it looks good at the funeral. It's not going to last, and it's not fooling anyone who is paying attention.

But the gospel of Christ is a real solution to our real problem, and communion with him lets us live our lives in the joy of being accepted by God, not for who we are but for who Jesus is. So the rehearsal of this little gospel drama is an important and practical way of experiencing friendship with the Son of God. It's not something done once when we first become Christians and then leave behind as we move on to more important matters. Jesus never tires of us coming to him with our sin; it only ever pleases and glorifies him when we do so. This is why Owen says, "This is every day's work; I know not how any peace can be maintained with God without it."[6]

Make time every day to stop and think carefully about these things. Examine your life and bring your sin to Jesus. Meditate on the love that moved him to die for your sins. Ponder his holiness and obedience and the righteousness he gives you as a gift. And then let your heart be full of delight and joy at the great exchange that has taken place. When that happens, your acceptance with God is achieving its purpose.

6 Owen, *Communion*, 318.

14

Looking to Him

WE NOW MOVE ON to the second way that we commune with Jesus in his purchased grace—our sanctification, or growth in holiness and obedience. It can be difficult to talk about sanctification without slipping into works righteousness (the idea that God accepts us because of our obedience to him). Part of the reason is the fact that, unlike in our justification (where God does all the work), we are called upon to be active participants in our own sanctification. And while we might pay lip service to the idea that in some sense we need God's grace to help us be holy, we oftentimes talk about it as if what matters most is the quality and consistency of our effort. Owen can provide a very helpful correction to some of the ways we think about this topic because he understands that our holiness does not find its strength and source in our effort but in the work of the Lord Jesus. Consider all that he does in order to make us holy.

First, he asks the Father to send the Holy Spirit to us. We cannot be sanctified without the presence of God's Spirit within us, and that presence is a gift that flows to us from the work of the Lord Jesus. He died to bring about the new covenant (Luke 22:20) that God had promised would bring his people obedient hearts (Jer. 31:31–34) and the presence of the Spirit within them (Ezek. 36:25–27). The crucified and risen Lord Jesus intercedes before the Father on our behalf, asking him to send the Holy Spirit to his people. This is what Jesus promised his disciples in John's Gospel: "I will ask the Father, and he will give you another Helper, to be with you forever, even the Spirit of truth, whom the world cannot receive, because it neither sees him nor knows him" (John 14:16–17).

Second, Jesus himself sends the Spirit to us. God the Father grants the request of his perfectly pleasing Son since he always hears Jesus's prayers (John 11:42). Jesus then sends his Spirit into our hearts to live there on his behalf and to accomplish his will in us. Jesus continually supplies us with all that we need through the Spirit, "drawing forth and exciting more effectual operations and actings of that indwelling Spirit."[1] This makes sense of what we see in the Bible, that the Spirit is sent to us *from* God the Father *by* God the Son (John 15:26). We might think of it this way: In response to the Son's request, God the Father gives the Spirit into his hand. The Son then sends the Spirit to his people in order to give them everything he has purchased on their behalf. The Spirit comes to us on Jesus's mission; he makes us spiritually alive, enlightens our darkened hearts and minds, and purifies our souls.

Third, Jesus bestows on us what Owen calls "habitual" grace. Before the gift of the Spirit, we were ruled by our sinful nature

---

1 John Owen, *Communion with the Triune God*, ed. Kelly M. Kapic and Justin Taylor (Wheaton, IL: Crossway, 2007), 325.

and its desires. Things like fits of anger, envy, drunkenness, and sexual immorality (Gal. 5:19–21) came easily to us; we didn't have to work at them, because they were natural to us. We did all those things by habit. But through the work of the Holy Spirit, the Lord Jesus has implanted a new nature and a new habit in our souls. Our eyes, which once were closed to the beauty of holiness and obedience, are now wide open. Our hearts, which were once hardened toward the Lord, are now soft and tender. Our souls, which used to delight in sin and self, are now captivated by the beauty of Jesus. All of this was purchased for us by the work of Jesus—his life, death, resurrection, and intercession.

In light of all that Jesus has done in order to make us holy—in our standing before God, in our external behaviors, and in the habit of our nature—we respond by communing with him. Speaking of God's people, Owen writes:

> They continually eye the Lord Jesus as the great Joseph, that has the disposal of all the granaries of the kingdom of heaven committed unto him; as one in whom it has pleased the Father to gather all things unto a head (Eph. 1:10), that from him all things might be dispensed unto them. All treasures, all fullness, the Spirit not by measure, are in him.[2]

Jesus is like a great king with an unending storehouse. His subjects can come to him for help time and time again, and they will never reach the end of his resources. He never needs to worry about overspending his "bank account" of love and grace for us.

2 Owen, *Communion*, 329–30.

In order to cultivate our friendship with Jesus in our sanctification, we need to look at three things in particular. First, we look to the purifying power of his blood. The more you grow as a Christian, the more aware you become of just how stained and impure your soul is because of sin. It's not just that our sin makes us guilty, though it does. The greater problem is that we are defiled in our souls. People are "unclean in their natures, unclean in their persons, unclean in their conversations; all rolled in the blood of their defilements; their hearts by nature a very sink, and their lives a dung hill."[3]

Since we know that nothing defiled can ever enter into the kingdom of heaven (Eph. 5:5), this awareness of our pollution in us drives us to Christ. Only his blood is able to cleanse us from all sin (1 John 1:7). His sacrifice has the power to make even the foulest sinner perfectly spotless. Communion with Jesus, then, means letting our minds dwell upon the power of his blood and the wonderful gift of being set free from the pollution of sin. Speaking of the purifying power of Jesus's blood, Owen says:

> Here faith obtains new life, new vigor, when a sense of vileness has even overwhelmed it. Here is a fountain opened: draw nigh, and see its beauty, purity, and efficacy. Here is a fountain laid of that work whose accomplishment we long for. One moment's communion with Christ by faith herein is more effectual to the purging of the soul, to the increasing of grace, than the utmost self-endeavors of a thousand ages.[4]

3 Owen, *Communion*, 330.
4 Owen, *Communion*, 331.

The second thing we need to see is what Owen calls "Christ's blood of sprinkling." The reference here is to the event recorded in the book of Exodus, where Moses sprinkled the people of Israel with the blood of sacrificed calves and goats. The point was that the application of the blood of a sacrifice would make the people ritually pure. And in a much greater and permanent way, the blood of Christ has the power to completely purify and cleanse our souls (Heb. 9:18–26). This means that one important way that we experience friendship with Jesus is by meditating carefully not just on the way that Jesus's blood takes away the penalty we deserve for our sin but also on the purifying power of his blood.

Finally, Owen tells us that believers commune with Jesus by looking to him as the one who gives us everything we need in order to be holy. The Spirit, sent to us by the risen Christ, sprinkles Christ's purifying blood on us and creates the holiness in us that we so desperately long for. He provides the outside assistance and power we lack, so we can confidently strive for holiness with all of our energy and power without ever finally relying on or investing our hope in our own efforts.

Were it not for Jesus, we would have no hope of ever being holy. Apart from him, the best we could hope for would be a religious program that we made up on our own, full of things like fasting and service and resolutions and promises to God. But we aren't left finally to look within ourselves for our sanctification. Instead, we have a solid anchor for our confidence that is outside of ourselves, the purchased grace of Jesus. So we strive for holiness with all our might, but we don't feel proud or self-satisfied, for we know that even the ability and desire to strive for godliness is a prize that Jesus purchased for us.

Notice that Owen understands that when it comes to our role in sanctification, the action begins in our mind. Holiness begins with your thoughts, with meditation and contemplation upon your own sin and need and inability, and also on the threefold promise of God—that the Spirit lives within you, that you have been given a new "habit of holiness," and that the Lord will assist you with all you need. There is no other hope for us, no other plan to make us holy, but none other is needed. Owen concludes, speaking of God's promises:

> Fix your soul here; you shall not tarry until you be ashamed. This is the way, the only way, to obtain full, effectual manifestations of the Spirit's dwelling in us; to have our hearts purified, our consciences purged, our sins mortified, our graces increased, our souls made humble, holy, zealous, believing—like to him; to have our lives fruitful, our deaths comfortable.[5]

5 Owen, *Communion*, 333.

15

In God's Family

WE COME NOW to the third and final way that we commune with Jesus in the grace he has purchased for us—the privileges we enjoy by virtue of his life, death, resurrection, and intercession. When we delight and rejoice in all that Jesus has secured for us, we are enjoying the heart of our friendship with him. Now, no book could possibly contain a list of all the good gifts that are ours in Christ, so we will have to be content to look at the chief blessing, the one from which all the others flow, namely, our adoption into God's family.

Imagine that you are called into the court of a good and powerful king. You are not looking forward to the experience, because you have been an outlaw and a traitor your whole life. You have violated his laws and been an enthusiastic member of a rebel group that has sought to overthrow the crown. You have no legitimate defense and no reason to hope for mercy. But when you appear for trial, you are stunned to discover that the king loves you and has decided to punish his beloved son in your place. As a result, you are declared innocent and treated as if you were a perfectly faithful subject of the king (that's the grace of acceptance that Owen talks about, our justification before God the King). But there's more, because this king also has the power to change your heart, so he takes away your insane and suicidal desire to rebel against him and replaces it with love and loyalty (that's the grace of sanctification). Because of the king's love for you, demonstrated clearly in the gift of his son, you never have to worry about finding yourself on the wrong end of the law again.

That's more than you could ever reasonably expect or demand, right? If that king merely let you go about your life from that point on, you would owe him your love and gratitude forever. But that's not nearly all that this king has in store for you. It is not enough for him to restore you to your status as a law-abiding citizen, because he ends your trial by declaring that he has adopted you into his family. You are no longer a criminal; you are not even a subject anymore. Instead, you are now a child of the king! You can see how that is the greatest blessing and honor that could possibly be bestowed upon you.

That small (and imperfect) analogy gives us a sense of what the Bible says has happened to us in Christ. We are no longer condemned criminals but have been adopted into the family of God:

> To all who did receive him, who believed in his name, he gave the right to become children of God, who were born, not of blood nor of the will of the flesh nor of the will of man, but of God. (John 1:12–13)

See what kind of love the Father has given to us, that we should be called children of God; and so we are. (1 John 3:1)

All who are led by the Spirit of God are sons of God. For you did not receive the spirit of slavery to fall back into fear, but you have received the Spirit of adoption as sons, by whom we cry, "Abba! Father!" The Spirit himself bears witness with our spirit that we are children of God. (Rom. 8:14–16)

If you think about the adoption of a child, at least five things need to be in place, and each of them is true of us in our status as God's children. First, the child needs to belong by right to another family; otherwise there would be no need for an adoption. And that was definitely the situation in our case. We were by nature children of wrath (Eph. 2:3), living in the domain of darkness (Col. 1:13). Satan was our spiritual father (John 8:44–47), and we were his loyal children.

The second element in any adoption is a second family, one to which the adoptee did not previously belong. For sinners, this is the family of God. We had no right or claim to be part of his household, for we were strangers and aliens from his people and promises (Eph. 2:11). Just as Adam was barred from going back into the garden of Eden after his sin (Gen. 3:24), so we have lost any right to approach God on a family basis.

The third part of an adoption is the legal and irrevocable transfer of the child from one family to the other. In the case of God's adopted children, this transfer was done in a public and authoritative way—declared to the angels (Luke 12:8–9; Eph. 3:10), to our former captor and master (Luke 11:21–22), and even to our own hearts (Gal. 4:6). God the Father has declared us to be his children (1 John 3:1–2), so Jesus is not ashamed to acknowledge us as his brothers and sisters (Heb. 2:11), and the Spirit of adoption has been poured into our hearts (Rom. 8:15) as proof of our new status. Our names have been deleted from Satan's contact list, and they've been written on God's family tree in permanent ink.

The fourth aspect of adoption is the child's freedom from all the obligations of the previous family. Before our adoption, we belonged to the family of those who had rebelled against God; our brothers and sisters were all the other people on earth who lived in opposition to God and his will. But now we have been set free from all those family bonds and obligations. Satan has no claim on our loyalty, and we do not need to listen to anything he says. We have been set free.

The final and most important element of an adoption is the granting of a new legal status to the child with all the rights and privileges that come with that status. Adoption isn't a half measure; an adopted child is placed on the same level and given the same standing as a natural-born one. So it is with those of us who have been graciously adopted as God's sons and daughters. We have been showered with incredible blessings and privileges. When we allow those privileges to shape our thoughts, emotions, and actions, we experience communion with the Lord Jesus.

To help us do just that, Owen sketches out four things that we receive by virtue of our adoption. First, we are given *liberty*. God gives his Spirit to his children, and where the Spirit is present, there is freedom (2 Cor. 3:17). Through the work of Christ, we have been set free from all the things that once plagued us: guilt, sin, death, and the condemnation that comes from God's law

(Gal. 5:1). A prince and princess can walk around their father's kingdom perfectly at ease, for they are only concerned to advance the family's agenda.

The liberty that we experience as adopted children transforms the way we think about our service and obedience. Think about it this way: if I were kidnapped and my captors forced me to split wood all day, I would be miserable. But I'll happily spend a day in my backyard splitting wood for my family. The knowledge that I'm serving the people I love and the prospect of long winter nights spent in front of the fireplace with my wife and kids make the work a delight. In the same way, the freedom we have as God's children makes our service to him an act of love and joy.

The second privilege we receive as God's children is a new *right*. We now have a legitimate claim to all the privileges and advantages that come with being part of the King's family. This includes all that the New Testament says we will inherit as adopted coheirs with Christ (Rom. 8:17): righteousness (Heb. 11:7), salvation (Heb. 1:14), and eternal life (Titus 3:7).

That brings us to the third privilege we want to consider, which is *boldness*. Imagine you were preparing to meet a very important person, the leader of your nation or a famous movie star or athlete. My guess is that you might be too intimidated to really enjoy the experience. I know I would be. But that person's children have no such concerns. They have an ease and boldness in their parent's presence because they are sure of their love. In the same way, we can draw near to the terrifying, holy God of the universe with boldness because he is our adoptive Father.

The final privilege we enjoy as God's adopted children is his *disciplinary correction*. This might not seem like much of a blessing;

in fact, no discipline is pleasant in the moment. But just like earthly parents correct their children for their own good, so our heavenly Father loves us too much to leave us on our own or without discipline.

These privileges, graciously purchased for us by the Lord Jesus, give shape to our friendship with him. Now, our obedience is a way that we live out our new status. We don't walk through our daily lives with the nagging anxiety of an orphan but in the confident knowledge that we have been made Jesus's honored brothers and sisters. When we suffer, we don't conclude that God no longer loves us, for we know that this is the way our older brother has himself walked (Heb. 5:8). Our relationship with Jesus is not cold and formal, but we are connected to him as part of his family.

PART 4

COMMUNION WITH THE SPIRIT

16

What Could Be Better?

HAVING DONE A DEEP DIVE on the friendship we have with God the Son, Owen now moves on to help us think through how we live in a relationship of love and friendship with the Holy Spirit. Owen is rightfully considered one of the church's greatest (and wordiest!) thinkers when it comes to the ministry of the Holy Spirit, so it might be surprising to learn how little of his book he devotes to the third person of the Trinity. But the explanation is simple: he had written so extensively on the Spirit in other places that he felt he could afford to be briefer in *Communion with God*.

Owen anchors his discussion of the Spirit in Jesus's words to his disciples on the night before his death. After warning them about the fierce opposition they will face from the world because they are his followers (John 15:18–25), he speaks pointedly about what the future holds for them: "They will put you out of the synagogues. Indeed, the hour is coming when whoever kills you will think he is offering service to God" (John 16:2). Now, if someone told you that you were going to have a target on your back and that the religious and civil authorities around you were going to hunt you down and attempt to kill you, you would figure that to be the worst news you'd hear that day.

Imagine the disciples' sadness then, when Jesus gave them some even worse news, telling them, "Now I am going to him who sent me" (John 16:5; see also 13:33). From our perspective a few thousand years later, we know that Jesus is referring to his upcoming bodily departure from earth, which took place when he ascended into heaven after his resurrection. The disciples, however, had no idea what Jesus was talking about, so they were understandably confused (John 13:36–37) and full of sorrow (John 16:6). Things couldn't get much worse—they were about to be persecuted, and the one person they could always count on to help them was announcing his plans to leave.

It must have seemed to the stunned disciples that things couldn't possibly be any worse, but that's not how Jesus saw it at all. That's why he said something shocking to them: "I tell you the truth: it is to your advantage that I go away" (John 16:7). You can see why the disciples would have trouble understanding how that could be the case; what could possibly be better than having Jesus with them? Think about what it meant to have Jesus in their lives; he was like a walking solution to all their problems. If they were hungry, he provided food (Mark 6:30–44). If they were in over their heads, he intervened (Mark 9:14–29). If they were in danger, he calmed the storm (Mark 4:35–41). If they were being criticized, he defended them (Mark 2:23–28). If they were confused, he explained things (Mark 4:10–20). Having Jesus around was like being at a wedding party every day (Mark 2:18–22), so how could it possibly be good news that he was leaving them?

The answer to that question is the gift of the Holy Spirit. Jesus says that it is good for him to leave, for "if I do not go away, the Helper will not come to you. But if I go, I will send him to you" (John 16:7). When it comes to describing how the Holy Spirit is sent to God's people, the Bible's teaching is complex. We are told that the Father sends the Spirit in Jesus's name (John 14:26), and also that Jesus sends the Spirit from the Father (John 15:26). As we saw in chapter 14 of this book, the gift of the Spirit comes to us by means of the grace that Jesus purchased for us. On the basis of his death, the risen and ascended Lord asks the Father to send the Spirit to his people, so he must leave his disciples in order to go to the Father and send the Holy Spirit to them. If Jesus goes, the Spirit comes. And, Jesus says, that's the best possible thing for his disciples.

Don't misunderstand—Jesus is not being polite or falsely modest. Remember that he prefaced his remarks by saying, "Nevertheless, I tell you the truth." He's being deadly serious. But even so, we may find ourselves in the same place as the disciples, struggling to make sense of Jesus's words. So perhaps we see our need to think carefully about what it means to have a relationship with God the Holy Spirit. We need to keep pressing until we can understand how the ministry of the Holy Spirit is even better than the bodily presence of the Lord Jesus. This is what Owen sets out to show us from Scripture in the final section of his book *Communion with God*. He writes:

> This is the sum: the presence of the Holy Ghost with believers as a comforter, sent by Christ for those ends and purposes for which he is promised, is better and more profitable for believers

than any *corporeal* presence of Christ can be, now [that] he has fulfilled the one sacrifice for sin which he was to offer.[1]

The key to understanding all that we are going to see here is the word that appears in John 16:7 to describe the work of the Holy Spirit. In the original Greek language in which John wrote, Jesus calls the Spirit the "paraclete." In the ancient world, calling someone a paraclete normally meant one of two things. Sometimes it meant that he was serving as an advocate, coming alongside others to help them when they are in need of protection, something like a modern defense attorney. Jesus himself is called our paraclete in this sense in one of John's letters: "If anyone does sin, we have an advocate [paraclete] with the Father, Jesus Christ the righteous" (1 John 2:1).

The other sense of the word *paraclete* is someone who provides comfort, like a good friend who walks with you in a time of need. And it seems from the surrounding context of Jesus's words in John 16 that this is the primary sense in which Jesus is using the word. Think about it—the disciples were about to face terrible persecution and danger. What they needed most was someone to strengthen and encourage them to face the trial without falling away under pressure (John 16:1). They needed a comforter.

And that's why the ministry of the Spirit is even better than having Jesus with us bodily. He brings to us the same kind of consolation and strength that Jesus would bring. That's why Jesus calls him "another Helper" in John 14:16. Jesus has been the disciples'

---

1   John Owen, *Communion with the Triune God*, ed. Kelly M. Kapic and Justin Taylor (Wheaton, IL: Crossway, 2007), 359.

source of divine strength and courage all along, and the Spirit will be another source of that very same comfort in their life. The Holy Spirit is the spirit of Christ (see Phil. 1:19; 1 Pet. 1:11), so his ministry is a continuation and application of the ministry of Christ. But while the Lord Jesus lived *with* the disciples during his earthly life, the Spirit will actually reside *inside* them. So Jesus says of the Spirit, "You know him, for he dwells with you and will be in you" (John 14:17). Having the Spirit live inside us is the greatest gift that the risen Christ gives to his people.

This is the truth that we are going to try to unpack in the coming chapters. But before we get there, it would be good to step back for a second and make sure that we don't miss the forest for the trees. The gift of the Spirit means that God is always present with us, just as Jesus promised (Matt. 28:20). He never leaves us, he never gets separated from us, he doesn't need to split his time between us and other believers. We will never know a moment of our lives when we are alone, without the help and strength that come with the Spirit's presence.

Think about what this means. The Father loves you so much that he sent his Son to come and save you. Jesus loves you also, so much that he laid down his life for you. So when the risen and ascended Jesus asked our loving heavenly Father for the very best gift he could possibly give us, the result was the sending of the Spirit. Now God is not just *with* us, but he is living *in* us. And the result of his presence in our lives is not what we might guess at first; he doesn't give us superhuman strength or X-ray vision; those things might be cool, but they are not what we need. Instead, God's presence brings weary sinners exactly what they need—everlasting comfort (2 Cor. 1:3).

17

Walking with the Spirit of Comfort

THE COMFORT WORK of the Holy Spirit is the foundation on which our friendship with him is constructed. In part 2 of this book, we saw how we carry out our friendship with God the Father in his love. In part 3, we looked at the communion we have with the God the Son in his grace. But when it comes to our relationship with the Holy Spirit, the most important thing to understand is the comfort he brings to us.[1] In order to understand his ministry more fully, we need to see three things: how he *comes to* believers, how he is *received by* believers, and how he *acts in the lives of* believers.

We have already discussed the fact that the Bible speaks of the Spirit as being sent to believers by both the Father (John

---

1 Based on the number of times he repeats the point, Owen would want me to remind you that he does not intend to talk much at all about the Spirit's role in our conversion. That is obviously a very important topic, but Owen's intention is to talk about the communion with the Spirit that we live out *after* we have become Christians.

14:16–17) and the Son (John 16:7). And that fact might lead us to conclude that the Holy Spirit is somehow relegated to third-class status in the Trinity, something like an employee who carries out his bosses' wishes. But to prevent that misunderstanding, Owen points us to something Jesus says to his disciples in John 15: "When the Helper comes, whom I will send to you from the Father, the Spirit of truth, who proceeds from the Father, he will bear witness about me" (John 15:26).

In this verse we see the activity of the Father and the Son, but we are also told that the Helper himself (the Spirit of truth) is engaged in the process. The Son asks and sends, the Father gives and sends, and the Spirit comes. That small detail reminds us of what Christians have always believed about the Holy Spirit, that he has his own will and identity; he is not a force or a principle but a person. He comes to us as the result of the Father's sending and the Son's work, but he also comes to us of his own liberty and on his own account. It is true that in order to carry out the plan for our salvation, the Holy Spirit condescends to be sent by the Father and Son. The Spirit doesn't remain at a distance from us, like a king who has no desire to be involved in the life of his subjects, but he stoops to serve as a comforter and helper to sinful and foolish people like you and me. But make no mistake—the Spirit is every bit as divine as the Father and the Son, so he enjoys the same sovereign power that they possess; he does whatever he wants to do. "The Father's and Son's sending of the Spirit does not derogate [detract] from his freedom in his workings, but he gives freely what he gives."[2]

2   John Owen, *Communion with the Triune God*, ed. Kelly M. Kapic and Justin Taylor (Wheaton, IL: Crossway, 2007), 370.

Here we must think carefully. How do we make sense of the fact that the three persons of the Trinity—Father, Son, and Holy Spirit—are each fully divine and equal in dignity, and yet we see what appears to be a hierarchy among them? Should we understand that the Father is greater than the Son, since he sent him into the world (John 3:16)? Does the fact that the Spirit is sent by the Father and Son indicate that he is inferior to them? We might be helped by a distinction that theologians make between the natures of the persons of the Trinity and the way they relate to one another in achieving our salvation. When thinking about the Spirit's willingness to be sent by the other persons of the Trinity, any "'inequality in respect of office' does [in] no way prejudice the equality of nature which he has with the Father and Son."[3] He comes freely to the believer because of what Owen calls "the conjunction and accord of his will with the gift of Father and Son."[4] The Spirit wants to come to us, and he is willing to be sent by the other persons of the Trinity.

The fact that the Spirit is completely equal with the Father and the Son means that we must be sure to show him the respect and honor he is due. Believers can and should pray to him. We should take great pains not to sin against him (e.g., Acts 5:3) or grieve him (Eph. 4:30), for "to sin against him is to sin against all the authority of God, all the love of the Trinity, and the utmost condescension of each person to the work of our salvation."[5] The presence of the Spirit is nothing less than the work of all three persons of the Trinity in us.

3 Owen, *Communion*, 363.
4 Owen, *Communion*, 362.
5 Owen, *Communion*, 363.

If the Spirit comes to us from the Father and the Son, what then is our role in receiving him? It's clear that when we first receive the Holy Spirit at our conversion, we actually don't have much of a role at all. Jesus compares the work of the Spirit to the wind, which no human can control or compel: "The wind blows where it wishes . . . so it is with everyone who is born of the Spirit" (John 3:8). When he comes to bring us to life (spiritually speaking), we are merely recipients, like a water glass being filled, or dry bones having life breathed into them (Ezek. 37:9–10). We do not do anything to earn or take hold of this wonderful gift.

That's how we first receive the Spirit. He comes to bring us to life and make us part of God's family by uniting us to Christ. We don't contribute anything to that process except our sin. But it should come as no surprise that this is not the way our daily communion with the Spirit works; you can't have a friendship where one person doesn't participate. There are things for us to do in order to experience and live out a relationship with the Spirit as our comfort. So Owen writes, "There is an active power to be put forth in his reception for consolation . . . and this is the power of faith."[6] The Spirit brings us comfort; we respond with faith.

What does that faith look like in practice then? Owen describes "three special acts of faith" that the believer can exercise to commune with the Spirit in his comfort:[7]

Faith *considers* the work that the Spirit was sent to do. We don't respond to the difficulties in our life as if we were orphans (John

6 Owen, *Communion*, 365.
7 Owen, *Communion*, 365.

14:18), but we remember and trust that we have been sent a wonderful source of comfort.

Faith *prays* for the Spirit's help and comfort (Luke 11:13). This asking God for the Spirit to give us the help and consolation we need "is the chief work of faith in this world."[8]

Faith *cherishes* the Spirit by being sensitive to his work and influence. When we love the Spirit, we are careful to walk in the ways that please him (Gal. 5:25) and believe the truths about God's love that he brings to bear on our soul (Rom. 5:5).

We live in constant need of the Spirit's comforting work. Even the best life is interrupted by sorrow, weakness, and sin. God's children sometimes experience dark periods of depression and grief. Sin and temptation never leave us alone, other people mistreat us, and sometimes we disappoint ourselves. In all those moments, faith looks past what we can see and feel in order to trust that we have been given the Spirit to bring us God's comfort.

Now, if we are being honest, there are times when that doesn't seem to work, where the consolation we long for doesn't seem to come. This is, in part, because we are able to refuse the Spirit's comfort. When he comes to give spiritual life to a sinner, he simply does his sovereign will without our effort or involvement. But his work of consolation is not like that; it involves our cooperation. Owen writes, "The Spirit as a sanctifier comes with power, to conquer an unbelieving heart; the Spirit as a comforter comes with

8 Owen, *Communion*, 366.

sweetness, to be received in a believing heart. He speaks, and we believe not that it is his voice; he tenders things of consolation, and we receive them not."[9]

The good news is that even when we do not feel the Spirit's comfort, he is always with us. Even when we feel overwhelmed by darkness and grief, and comfort feels far away, we can be sure that the Spirit is there with us. He is not in any way limited, his love never runs out, and he's never distracted or stretched too thin to help us in our time of need. We can be sure that the Spirit's comfort will never fail us even if our ability to perceive it sometimes does.

9   Owen, *Communion*, 367.

18

Pouring Out God's Love

WHAT DOES IT LOOK like when the Spirit is at work to comfort us? What kinds of things should we expect him to do in us and for us? This question gets to the "nuts and bolts" of our communion with the Holy Spirit, so in this chapter we will look at what the Spirit accomplishes in us. Owen's approach here is simply to walk through the Bible and notice what it says in this regard, so we will follow him on that path and see five things about the work of the Spirit along the way.

First, the Spirit brings to mind the things of Christ, just as Jesus had promised the disciples in John 14:26. This is a great source of comfort to us, for the Spirit brings to the minds of believers the precious promises that Jesus made to us. The Spirit is responsible for "whatever peace, relief, comfort, joy, [and] supportment we have at any time received from any work, promise, or thing done by Christ."[1] If you've ever been comforted in a difficult time by

---

1   John Owen, *Communion with the Triune God*, ed. Kelly M. Kapic and Justin Taylor (Wheaton, IL: Crossway, 2007), 375.

the words of Christ, that was the work of the Spirit bringing consolation to you. And because the Spirit does this work of comfort with divine power, he is capable of bringing the words of Christ to bear in our hearts in even the most upsetting situations. Through the Spirit, "comfort from the words and promises of Christ sometimes break in through all the opposition into the saddest and darkest condition imaginable; it comes and makes men sing in a dungeon, rejoice in flames, glory in tribulation; it will [come] into prisons, racks, through temptations, and the greatest distresses imaginable."[2]

Second, the Spirit comforts us by pouring the Father's love into our hearts (Rom. 5:5). As we have already seen in part 2, the Father loves us; he accepts us, adopts us, and only ever intends to do good to us for all eternity. But at times it can be hard for us to feel as if that is true. The cares of life in a fallen world often seem more real and urgent than the love of God. Struggles with sin tempt us to think that God couldn't possibly love us as much as the Bible says he does. But when we find ourselves in that situation, the Spirit is able to comfort our souls by persuading us of the Father's love for us in Christ.

One Sunday when our church was singing about the greatness of God's grace (greater even than all our sin), I was suddenly struck by the fact that those words we were singing were really true. Now on one level, that was not a shocking revelation; I already knew that God's word proclaims that his love overcomes our sin. But in that moment, I found myself really believing it. I felt it deep in my soul, so much so that I leaned over to my friend in the middle

2   Owen, *Communion*, 375.

of the song and said excitedly, "Did you know that this is *really* true?" In that moment, the Spirit was pouring God's love into my heart. He was convincing me at the deepest level of all that I already knew. The Spirit was bringing me comfort.

Third, the Spirit bears witness with our spirit that we are children of God (Rom. 8:16). As we've already seen, we have been adopted out of sin and death and into God's family. But there are times when a discouraged, doubting, or depressed Christian might wonder if he or she really *does* belong to God. A believer's conscience and sense of indwelling sin might cause him to fear that he does not actually belong to God. "Satan, in the meantime, opposes with all his might; sin and law assist him; many flaws are found in his evidences [reasons for thinking that he really is God's adopted child]; the truth of them all is questioned; and the soul hangs in suspense as to the issue."[3] In that situation, the Spirit "bears witness" on the believer's behalf. He is able to speak to the believer's heart with some kind of powerful sense or word of consolation and comfort to convince him that he belongs to God. This is a wonderful way to have communion with the Spirit.

The fourth thing the Spirit does is seal us (Eph. 1:13). We don't really use seals very often in our world, so this image might be a little strange to us. But in biblical times (and in Owen's day), seals were used to secure important certificates and contracts. Wax was dripped onto the document, and an engraved seal was used to make an impression in the soft wax. That's an appropriate picture, because the ministry of the Spirit is to form the image of God in us by making us more and more like Jesus (Rom. 8:29).

3 Owen, *Communion*, 379.

When a document was sealed, it was a way of making the matter official and irrevocable, something like our modern notary. When someone set his seal to his court testimony or legal document, it could not be changed. Once the wax hardened, there was no going back. So when God promises us forgiveness of our sins, the salvation of our souls, and eternal life with him in heaven, he seals us with his Spirit. He puts his stamp on our souls so that we can have certainty that we will receive all that he has intended to give us. You can see how this is a source of great comfort and confidence for God's people. As we see the image of Christ being formed in us by the Spirit, it "gives us a persuasion of our being separated and set apart for God, [and] we have a communion with him therein."[4]

The fifth thing the Spirit does for us is serve as a down payment on all that we will inherit from God. In America when people sign a contract to buy a house, they will normally leave a deposit of some sort to show that they are serious about carrying the transaction through to completion. That's a picture of the way the Spirit brings comfort to his people. His presence with us confirms God's promises and shows that he is completely committed to doing all that he has said that he will do.

If you stop to think about it, it is incredibly kind and loving of the Father to give us such a deposit. After all, we have no good reason to doubt his promises; he has told us about them clearly in his word, and he has never failed to do what he says. But he knows our weakness and that it can be hard for us to carry our trust into the future. And since he does not want us to live in fear

---

4   Owen, *Communion*, 382.

and uncertainty, he sent his Spirit so that we will have a witness within us.

The presence of the Spirit also gives us an important clue to what our inheritance will be like. A deposit is usually made up of the same thing as the whole that it represents. The down payment on a house is made with money because the house will be purchased with money. In the same way, God sends the Spirit to live within us because our inheritance will be a much greater and fuller experience of God's presence and glory. Life with the Spirit now is preparing us and making us ready for eternal life.

What a marvelous gift the Holy Spirit is to believers! His ministry to us is one of love, kindness, and mercy. He represents God's intention not just to save you, but to hold direct communion with you. The Father loves you, and he wants you to know it. He has a wonderful inheritance in store for you, and he wants you to live now with confidence and joy. Owen summarizes it this way:

> The Comforter gives a sweet and plentiful evidence and persuasion of the love of God to us, such as the soul is taken, delighted, satiated with. This is his work, and he does it effectually. To give a poor sinful soul *a comfortable persuasion*, affecting it throughout, in all its faculties and affections, that God in Jesus Christ loves him, delights in him, is well pleased with him, has thoughts of tenderness and kindness toward him; to give, I say, a soul an overflowing sense hereof, is an inexpressible mercy.[5]

5   Owen, *Communion*, 378.

19

Taught by the Spirit

CENTURIES BEFORE Jesus was born, the prophet Isaiah spoke about the relationship between the coming Messiah and the Spirit of God:

> And the Spirit of the LORD shall rest upon him,
>   the Spirit of wisdom and understanding,
>   the Spirit of counsel and might,
>   the Spirit of knowledge and the fear of the LORD.
>   (Isa. 11:2)

Isaiah saw that the deliverer God was sending to his people would be marked by the Holy Spirit's resting or remaining upon him. He would be a man marked by the Spirit's constant presence in his life, and the result would be that he would have a never-ending source of "wisdom and understanding . . . counsel and . . . knowledge."

And that's exactly what we see when we look at the beginning of Jesus's public ministry. At his baptism the Spirit descended on him (Luke 3:22), and then "full of the Holy Spirit" he went out into the desert to overcome the devil's temptations (Luke 4:1). As soon as those temptations were ended, Jesus went "in the power of the Spirit" (Luke 4:14) to teach in Galilee. When he arrived in Nazareth, he opened the book of Isaiah in the synagogue and taught them that "the Spirit of the Lord is upon me . . . to proclaim good news" (Luke 4:18).

Because the Holy Spirit was with him, Jesus had a unique ability to understand the things of God—his will, his ways, and the meaning of his word. As a result, he was able to preach with a wisdom and authority that astonished the people of his day (Luke 4:32); they simply had never heard someone proclaim God's truth with such insight and clarity. It is not an exaggeration to say that Jesus's entire ministry of teaching people the ways of God was carried out through the power of the Spirit's presence with him (Acts 1:2).

The Spirit's empowering of Jesus for his ministry is sometimes referred to as an anointing (e.g., Luke 4:18 and Acts 10:38). To *anoint* is to smear or rub with oil, and in the Old Testament it was a way of setting someone apart for a certain office (like a king) or ministry (like a priest or a prophet). And that's exactly what the Spirit did. His presence marked Jesus as the one sent by God, and his power enabled him to carry out the work he had been sent to do. That is an amazing truth to try to wrap your mind around. The Son of God in human flesh was equipped with wisdom and understanding by the Spirit of God.

And that's not the end of the story. Shockingly enough, the Bible tells us that the Spirit has a similar role to play in *our* lives. You and I are not God's Messiah (I hope that's not a surprise to you), but we do have the same Spirit dwelling in us and working in us. We also are anointed by the Spirit. So the apostle John writes to the church, "But you have been anointed by the Holy One, and you all have knowledge" (1 John 2:20). And again, "The anointing that you received from him abides in you, and you have no need that anyone should teach you. . . . His anointing teaches you about everything, and is true, and is no lie" (1 John 2:27). This is why Jesus had promised his disciples that the Spirit would teach them (John 14:26) and guide them in all truth (John 16:13).

Our experience of this anointing begins at our conversion, where the Spirit makes us alive to the things of God and convicts us of our sin (John 16:8). The Spirit works powerfully through the preaching of God's word to bring us to faith and help us to understand the gospel. But our relationship with the Spirit is not primarily a matter of facts and data points. It is true that we need facts; you cannot have a relationship with God unless you know the truth about him and what he has done to save us in Christ. But as Owen has been showing us, our friendship with the Holy Spirit is carried out when those facts are made a source of comfort and consolation to our souls.

It is a sad thing when Christians know and believe the truth about God's love for them but receive little comfort from that knowledge. It's like having a world-class symphony play a Mozart composition for someone who is hard of hearing. It's like having a "Michelin star" chef make an exquisite meal for someone whose tongue is numb. There's nothing wrong with the gospel, but sometimes we lack the capacity to enjoy and appreciate its beauty.

That's where the ministry of the Spirit comes in. He helps us to appreciate and delight in the truths of the gospel. He works in us the ability to have some sense of just how good the good news really is. He teaches us the truth of God through the word and then makes us able to rejoice in it. So Owen writes, "We have this, then, by the Spirit: he teaches us of the love of God in Christ; he makes every gospel truth as wine well refined to our souls, and the good things of it to be a feast of fat things—gives us joy and gladness of heart with all that we know of God."[1]

Can you see how this ministry of the Holy Spirit is essential to our friendship with God? Friends enjoy one another; they find one another's company to be a source of delight. And in his relentless kindness, God is not content just to save us; he wants to change us by his Spirit so we can hear the beautiful symphony of his love. He would transform our tastes so we can enjoy the exquisite flavors of his grace.

This is one of the ways that God keeps us close to him and preserves us in our faith. We generally stick close to whatever delights us, and if we find no more cause for happiness in the truth of the gospel than we do in some sort of false teaching, then we are liable to fall into error. But the more we know the gospel's "power, sweetness, joy, and gladness,"[2] the less likely we are to be seduced by the bland or bitter alternatives that the world offers to us. We live out our friendship with the Spirit by pursuing this delight and being sensitive when he leads us and prompts us toward it. "When we find any of the good truths of the gospel come

---

1 John Owen, *Communion with the Triune God*, ed. Kelly M. Kapic and Justin Taylor (Wheaton, IL: Crossway, 2007), 387.

2 Owen, *Communion*, 387.

home to our souls with life, vigor, and power, giving us gladness of heart, transforming us into the image and likeness of it—the Holy Ghost is then at his work."[3]

One of the most important ways that we can seek and enjoy this ministry of the Spirit is through prayer. When we pray, we are enjoying one of the chief privileges that comes to us through the gospel. In prayer, we come into the presence of God as his friends to talk with him and unburden our hearts to him. There we can get a taste of the gospel's sweetness, as we take the things that tempt us to fear and anxiety and lay them at his feet, confident that he cares for us (1 Pet. 5:7). In prayer, believers "sweetly ease our hearts in the bosom of the Father, and receive in refreshing tastes of his love. The soul is never more raised with the love of God than when by the Spirit taken into intimate communion with him in the discharge of this duty."[4]

Now, if you're like me, Owen's description of a Christian's delight in prayer might tempt you to discouragement. Sometimes I feel like I'm lousy at praying. I don't know exactly what to say. The words that come to me aren't really adequate for the situation, my heart doesn't always sync up to the truth I know, and my mind wanders off of God and onto the things I've been praying about. So it feels like bad news to say that my communion with the Spirit is oftentimes experienced in and conducted through the Spirit.

But what if I told you that one of the ways the Spirit is a friend to us is helping us when we pray? This is exactly what the apostle Paul wrote to the church at Rome:

3 Owen, *Communion*, 387–88.
4 Owen, *Communion*, 388.

The Spirit helps us in our weakness. For we do not know what to pray for as we ought, but the Spirit himself intercedes for us with groanings too deep for words. And he who searches hearts knows what is the mind of the Spirit, because the Spirit intercedes for the saints according to the will of God. (Rom. 8:26–27)

This means that the Spirit is at work in our prayers, weak though they may be. When we don't know what to pray for, the Spirit always intercedes according to the will of God. Even when our words fail us and our prayers are reduced to inarticulate groaning (Rom. 8:23), the Spirit knows just what to say on our behalf. So prayer follows the pattern of the gospel. God has done everything necessary to bring us into a relationship with him; he makes up for our weakness and inadequacy. God has given us his Spirit so that prayer is not a burden but an opportunity to taste the sweetness of his love for us in Christ.

20

The Spirit's Ministry

IN THE PREVIOUS couple of chapters, we have seen the wonderful works of the Holy Spirit in our lives: he brings the promises of God to our minds, he pours the love of God into our hearts, he convinces us that we are God's children, he seals us for the coming day of redemption, he serves as a guarantee of our future inheritance, and he teaches us to delight in our salvation, making us able to pray to God with joy. In response, our hearts are moved to worship the Holy Spirit and thank the Father and the Son for this wonderful gift!

In this chapter, let's build on what we have seen by thinking about some of the effects of the Spirit's ministry in our lives. If the Holy Spirit does all the things we've just mentioned, what results should we expect to see produced in our lives? Owen suggests that we can think about them under four headings: comfort, hope, peace, and joy.

First is *comfort*, that sense of rest and contentedness we can have in our souls, even when we are experiencing trials and difficulties.

This is a particular work of the Holy Spirit. Every time the Bible mentions believers being comforted (and it comes up pretty frequently), it comes in some way as the result of the Spirit's involvement. In Acts 9, for example, we read about the early church: "So the church throughout all Judea and Galilee and Samaria had peace and was being built up. And walking in the fear of the Lord and *in the comfort of the Holy Spirit*, it multiplied" (Acts 9:31).

Think about what it means that God has provided comfort or consolation for us through the Holy Spirit. It must mean that he knows that this life is going to be full of sadness, sorrow, and difficulty for his people. After all, you only need comfort when things are difficult; you don't console the winner, but the loser. You don't comfort the healthy person, but the sick. The Spirit is particularly God's gift to us in all the things that make life in this fallen world so painful—our sin, the weakness of our faith, the fragility of our bodies, the difficulties of our relationships with other people.

The good news is that the comfort the Spirit brings to us is powerful and strong. Our troubles, after all, are awfully tough; the world we live in is cursed, broken, and infected by sin. In our folly, we are prone to making our problems worse. In light of all of that, no weak, flimsy, or fragile comfort is going to last very long. But the Spirit gives us "strong encouragement" when we look to him in our troubles. Because he is strong, the comfort he gives "confirms, corroborates, and strengthens the heart under any evil; it fortifies the soul, and makes it able cheerfully to undergo anything that it is called unto."[1] It is for this reason that the apostle

1   John Owen, *Communion with the Triune God*, ed. Kelly M. Kapic and Justin Taylor (Wheaton, IL: Crossway, 2007), 393.

Paul says that believers have an "eternal comfort" (2 Thess. 2:16), for our consolation is unshakably founded on eternal love, eternal redemption, and an eternal inheritance.

You can see why the Spirit is called the Comforter; everything he does in us is aimed at giving us consolation in a fallen world. Without him, we are left like orphans. But with him, we are convinced that we are God's children. Without him, we are overwhelmed by our sin. But with him, we are conformed to the image of Christ. Without him, we are without hope in the world. But with him, we are sure of the inheritance we will one day receive.

In that way, the comfort of the Spirit is closely related to the *hope* he produces in us. This is what Paul prayed for the church in Rome: "May the God of hope fill you with all joy and peace in believing, *so that by the power of the Holy Spirit you may abound in hope*" (Rom. 15:13). Hope looks forward; it is a belief about the future that controls the way we feel about the present. And much of the ministry of the Spirit is aimed at convincing us that God has good plans for us down the road.

Imagine that a wealthy relative of yours died and left you an incredible fortune. As is sometimes the case in such matters, there was legal red tape that meant you couldn't take possession of your inheritance immediately; you had to wait for it. Now imagine that some kind of financial trouble came your way, maybe you lost your job, or your home needed a very expensive repair. In that scenario, would you be upset and anxious about your troubles? Would you be overwhelmed by sorrow and despair? Would you panic and conclude that all is lost? Of course not! The sure hope of a future inheritance would be a source of comfort to you in your present financial difficulties. You would know that you could endure the present, momentary trouble because you had a future, permanent solution. You would be able to face your problems without fear or despair because you would know that everything would be fine in the end.

In the same way, the Spirit provides hope by giving us a sense of God's love and provision. He assures us of all that we will one day receive from the Father as his adopted children. As believers, we can face whatever trials and difficulties come our way in light of the hope that the Spirit produces in us.

In addition to comfort and hope, the Spirit also produces *peace* in his people. We see this promised in John's Gospel where Jesus said to his disciples, "But the Helper, the Holy Spirit, whom the Father will send in my name, he will teach you all things and bring to your remembrance all that I have said to you. Peace I leave with you; my peace I give to you. Not as the world gives do I give to you. Let not your hearts be troubled, neither let them be afraid" (John 14:26–27).

Jesus doesn't want his disciples to be afraid or troubled, so he promises them peace. And how does that peace come into their lives? Only through the ministry and presence of the Holy Spirit. Peace is one of the fruits he bears in his people (Gal. 5:22), and to set our minds on him is "life and peace" (Rom. 8:6). Because we have the Spirit, we have a "comfortable persuasion" in our "soul and conscience" that we are accepted by God as his friends in Christ.[2]

Finally, the Spirit brings *joy* to his people (Rom. 14:17). Oftentimes he does this by bringing to our minds all that we have

2 Owen, *Communion*, 394.

received in Christ. Who can contemplate all that the Lord has prepared for us (1 Cor. 2:9) and not feel some sense of joy? Other times, the Spirit produces joy directly in our souls without using any kind of external cause. He is like a well of joy living inside of us, and in his sovereign kindness, the Spirit sometimes simply produces in our soul a great happiness and delight in the Lord and in his love. Just like he made John the Baptist leap for joy in Elizabeth's womb (Luke 1:41–44), he can cause our souls to feel suddenly overjoyed at our salvation. Owen describes the Spirit's work like this: "He secretly infuses and distils it [joy] into the soul, prevailing against all fears and sorrows, filling it with gladness, exultations; and sometimes with unspeakable raptures of mind."[3]

What a gift to have this kind of relationship with God the Spirit! Again, we must remember that nothing forces God to treat us with such kindness; it is simply his love and care that causes his Spirit to treat us in this way. Just imagine having a friend who leaves you feeling comfort, peace, joy, and hope every time you get together. Now imagine that this friend is willing to be with you constantly, always available to help you in every circumstance. That's a small taste of what it means to have communion with God the Holy Spirit. He is an ever-present, all-powerful, never-failing source of love and comfort to God's people. He works to seal and confirm our inheritance so that we can live with hope and joy as we look to the future.

---

3 Owen, *Communion*, 395.

21

He's the Real Thing

IT'S BASICALLY IMPOSSIBLE to overstate how wonderful the Spirit's friendship is. Jesus had no greater promise for his disciples than that he would send the Spirit to help them. The Spirit is the good gift that the loving Father gives to his children (Luke 11:13) and the spring of living water welling up within God's people to refresh and strengthen them (John 7:38–39). His permanent presence with God's people is one of the greatest and most glorious advantages that New Testament believers have over those in the Old Testament era. "Ordinary" Christians, with the Spirit dwelling in them, have a more privileged experience of God's love and presence than any of their Old Testament "heroes" would have had (that seems to be at least part of Paul's point in 2 Corinthians 3:7–18). Without the Spirit, there are no pastors (Acts 20:28) and no church members gifted to serve the body (1 Cor. 12:4–11). Owen isn't exaggerating when he says that "the whole religion we profess, without the administration of the Spirit, is nothing. . . . In our worship of and obedience to God, in our own consolation, sanctification, and the ministerial [pastoral] employment, the Spirit is the principle, the life, soul, the all of the whole."[1]

Since all of that is true, it should come as no surprise that the Spirit's work is often under attack in our world. Between satanic obstruction and the hatred of wicked people, there is no shortage of opposition lined up to frustrate (if it were possible) the purposes of the Spirit. So as we think about just how great it is to have a relationship with God the Spirit, we need to take a moment to think carefully about the ways we might be tempted to get off course. To that end, Owen discusses two ways that people who would claim to be followers of Jesus might find themselves unwittingly opposing the Spirit's work.

One way that we might oppose the Spirit is through what Owen calls "private contempt." This is seen in people who claim to be Christians but are suspicious and critical of anyone who seems to care too much about the Spirit's work. The apostle Paul tells us to be zealous for the Spirit's gifts, but many professing Christians can't be bothered to even ask for that; they wouldn't know what to do with those gifts if they got them. The Spirit simply has nothing to do with the lives of these people; they take comfort and consolation in their own morality and their achievements rather than in the Spirit whom God gives to his children.

At the other extreme, some professing Christians are only interested in what seem to be spectacular manifestations of the Spirit's power. They go on and on about miraculous powers, speaking in tongues, prophetic knowledge, and supernatural healing, but

1   John Owen, *Communion with the Triune God*, ed. Kelly M. Kapic and Justin Taylor (Wheaton, IL: Crossway, 2007), 398.

they have little concern for the holiness, humility, and love for Christ that are the real hallmarks of his ministry.

Another way that we can go astray is through what Owen terms "the public contempt of the Spirit." We see this contempt in churches in which worship is carried out without any of the gifts and graces that the Holy Spirit gives to his people. Picture in your mind a church gathering where a pastor who has no relationship with God reads out a cold, formal, elaborate, and meaningless (to the people in attendance) form of worship. This church might claim that the words they read together are ancient and well-written, but the gospel message is not preached or delighted in there.

Now picture in your mind a very different kind of church gathering. This one has a tremendous show. The music is loud and energetic, the message is always positive and inspiring, and the videos, lighting, and facility are professional grade. Understandably, lots of visitors crowd the church each week. The problem is that the gospel is not at the heart of the church. It could be that the leadership of the church wouldn't go so far as to deny the gospel message, but that message really doesn't have much to do with the life of the church. Instead, the goal is to help people live happy lives here and now.

Those two imagined churches are caricatures of two ways that people who claim to be followers of Christ can unknowingly show contempt for the Holy Spirit. What these churches do when they gather on Sundays does not require the presence, power, and help of the Holy Spirit at all; the results that they achieve can be done completely in their own strength. In these kinds of churches, pastors who minister a simple gospel in the power of the Spirit (like the apostle Paul did; see 1 Corinthians 2:2–4) are simply not welcome. If there is worship happening in these churches, it is not worship inspired by the Spirit of Christ (cf. 1 Tim. 4:1).

So if all that is true, then how can we know the real thing? How can we tell whether our lives and our churches are on the right track? How can we evaluate people and ministries that claim to be led by the Spirit? Those were urgent questions in John Owen's day, and they may be even more pressing now. The apostle John instructs us: "Beloved, do not believe every spirit, but test the spirits to see whether they are from God, for many false prophets have gone out into the world" (1 John 4:1). Owen suggests four things to look for as we "test the spirits"; these things should be no surprise to us by now, but it is helpful to see them fleshed out.

First, the Holy Spirit *brings to mind the words of Christ*. He inspired the writing of the Bible so that we would have Christ's words, and now he helps believers by reminding us of and helping us to understand them. This is a helpful way to evaluate anyone's teaching ministry. If a teacher encourages you to read, understand, and believe God's word, that's a very good sign. If a teacher claims to have new revelations, new insights, or new teaching, you should be extremely skeptical. A person who is walking in step with the Spirit will lead people to, never away from, the word that the Spirit has inspired.

Second, *the Spirit glorifies Christ*. This is what Jesus told us to expect: "He will glorify me, for he will take what is mine and declare it to you" (John 16:14). Jesus didn't come to glorify himself but to glorify the Father who sent him (John 8:50). In the same way, the Holy Spirit doesn't seek his own glory but the glory of Christ. In order to accomplish that purpose, he makes Jesus "glorious, honorable, and of high esteem in the hearts of believers."[2] We can evaluate ourselves and others using this simple test: Do our words and actions glorify Christ? Someone whose life and ministry are marked by the Holy Spirit will tend not toward their own glory but that of the Lord Jesus.

Third, *the Spirit pours the love of God into the hearts of his people.* He fills us "with joy, peace, and hope [Rom. 15:13]; quieting and refreshing the hearts of them in whom he dwells; giving them liberty and rest, confidence, and the boldness of children."[3] False teachers tend to do just the opposite. They enslave people with heavy burdens, telling them that God's love and favor depend on their obedience, or the strength and purity of their faith, or the amount of money they give. The spirit abroad in our world is "a spirit of cruelty and reproach towards others," but the Spirit of Christ is "a spirit of adoption and consolation."[4]

Finally, *the Spirit leads believers to pray.* As we have seen, the Spirit is a close friend to believers when we pray (Rom. 8:26). His ministry convicts us of sin and prevents us from relying on ourselves. He leads us to the throne of grace in prayer and helps us to ask our loving Father for all we need. Beware of anyone who thinks that humble prayer is too simple a way of communing with God; we never graduate beyond the need for prayer.

These are very helpful ways to make sure that the spirit with whom we have a relationship is the Spirit of Christ and not the spirit of the world. Following Christ is not easy, and life will bring us many troubles (John 16:33). But when people are experiencing

2 Owen, *Communion,* 401.
3 Owen, *Communion,* 402.
4 Owen, *Communion,* 402.

the Spirit, they will know rest, love, and freedom. The desire of their heart, however imperfectly it may be executed at times, will be for the glory of Christ. Obedience will be their delight, for they delight in God's word and take their identity from being part of God's household. They will resort to prayer frequently, for the Spirit drives them to bring all their requests to God. How kind and gracious the Spirit is to us!

22

The Spirit Who Stoops

OUR ENJOYMENT OF our relationship with God the Holy Spirit is in some ways dependent on how highly we value who he is and what he does for us. If we have little sense of how to identify his work in our lives and little appreciation for the things he produces in us, then we will not think much of his friendship. Therefore, in order to raise our hearts up and fit us for the privilege and duty of communing with the Spirit, Owen helps us to think carefully about the comfort he brings to us.

Particularly, we should consider *what the Spirit comforts us against*. As we've said before, comfort is only needed when something is particularly painful or difficult. So what things in our lives require the Spirit's ministry of comfort? It's almost an overwhelming question to ask, given all the challenges and suffering in the world. But when we look to Scripture, we can identify three kinds of suffering that draw out the Spirit's comfort.

First, the Spirit comforts us when we are afflicted. The book of Hebrews speaks to us about the difficulties and pains appointed for God's children:

And have you forgotten the exhortation that addresses you as sons?

"My son, do not regard lightly the discipline of the Lord,
    nor be weary when reproved by him.
For the Lord disciplines the one he loves,
    and chastises every son whom he receives."
      (Heb. 12:5–6)

No one likes pain and trouble; we all naturally avoid it. But in the same way that a loving father disciplines his children, so God sometimes corrects, protects, and shapes us through troubles and suffering (see the way Paul describes his experience in 2 Corinthians 11:7–10).

But the danger, according to Hebrews, is that we will either "regard lightly" or "be weary" when this discipline appears in our lives. We do this when we fail to see the problems in our lives as coming from God's hand, and we sink into despair and fail to benefit from them in the way that we should. Often when we are faced with some sort of trouble—an illness, a loss, a persistent weakness, or a difficult relationship—our temptation can either be to "take no notice of God in it" or be so distraught that we "sink under the weight."[1]

The person who misses the point of his suffering and the one who simply sinks under the weight of it both miss out on the comfort and benefits that the Holy Spirit will bring to believers in their troubles. The apostle Paul was able to say, "We rejoice in

1 John Owen, *Communion with the Triune God*, ed. Kelly M. Kapic and Justin Taylor (Wheaton, IL: Crossway, 2007), 406.

our sufferings" (Rom. 5:3) because "God's love has been poured into our hearts through the Holy Spirit" (Rom. 5:5). Paul could face trials with joy and confidence because the Spirit comforted him with the knowledge of God's love. The Spirit made Paul sure that everything in his life, including his suffering, came to him from the hand of his loving heavenly Father. As a result, he was able to trust the Lord's good plan and purpose in it. If we hope to benefit from the Lord's discipline and training, we will need the Spirit's comfort.

Second, we need the Spirit's comfort when we feel overwhelmed by the burden of our sin. Satan's accusations (Rev. 12:10), our consciences, and the holiness of God's law can sometimes combine to fill our hearts with a sense of guilt and condemnation. We might begin to feel that we cannot possibly be God's children, or we might fear that he is angry at us because of our sin. In those moments and seasons of life, when we might be overwhelmed by despair or even tempted to give up, the Spirit comforts us, assuring us that God's love has never depended on our goodness and persuading us that we are his beloved children. Sin might work to destroy our soul's sense of peace, but the Spirit is up to the task of bringing us comfort. He enables the sin-plagued soul to flee to Christ for genuine refuge (Heb. 6:18).

Third, the Spirit brings us consolation in our obedience to God. Growing in holiness can be exhausting, hard work. The New Testament uses words like "strive" (Heb. 12:14), "put to death" (Rom. 8:13), and "cut . . . off" (Matt. 5:30) to describe what it looks like. For that reason, some believers will experience a temptation to "grow weary in doing good" (2 Thess. 3:13), while others will be tempted to pride when they see growth in their lives. In both those cases, the Spirit's comfort is essential so that we may continue in obedience "cheerfully, willingly, patiently to the end."[2]

The Spirit comforts us in our afflictions, our sin, and our pursuit of obedience; that's pretty much everything, isn't it? The Spirit brings a flood of relief and comfort to the souls of suffering and sin-sick Christians by persuading them of the unending and unchanging love of their heavenly Father. He strengthens our hearts and souls in our time of trial and temptation by reminding us of all that we have received by the grace of Jesus.

Thinking about this inspires Owen to some of his most delightful writing, and it's worth quoting him at length. He imagines the self-talk of a Spirit-comforted soul:

> The world *hates* me . . . but my *Father* loves me. Men despise me as a *hypocrite*; but my Father loves me as a *child*. I am *poor* in this world; but I have a *rich* inheritance in the love of my Father. I am *straitened* [deprived] in all things; but there is *bread enough* in my Father's house. I *mourn* in secret under the power of my lusts and sin, where no eyes see me; but the Father sees me, and is full of compassion. With a sense of his kindness, which is better than life, I rejoice in tribulation, glory in affliction, triumph as a conqueror. Though I am killed all the day long, all my sorrows have a *bottom* that may be fathomed—my trials, *bounds* that may be compassed; but the *breadth*, and *depth*, and *height* of the love of the Father, who can express?[3]

2 Owen, *Communion*, 407.
3 Owen, *Communion*, 409.

This is so much better than the comfort the world can offer us, with its thin appeals to self-love and self-acceptance, the distracting pleasures of sin, and the emptiness of momentary pleasures. Real comfort for our souls is found only in what the Spirit of God gives us. He reminds us that great as they may seem, our problems and failures are limited; they will come to an end one day. And he convinces us that the love of God the Father and the grace of Jesus will always be with us.

Before we move on, it is worth stopping to consider *why* the Spirit does his work of comforting us. After all, it's not like we have done anything to deserve his care and love; rather, we have been "froward [difficult], perverse, unthankful; grieving, vexing, provoking him."[4] We have taken the Spirit for granted and failed to respond in loving obedience to his promptings. As a result, his ministry to us surely cannot be rooted in anything in us.

The only conclusion that makes any sense is that he is motivated by his own kindness and compassion to stoop down and care for us. He sees us in our sin and suffering, and full of compassion he moves toward us. He is not compelled to comfort us by some force outside himself; he is not reluctant in any way to bring God's blessings to us. Owen writes of the source of the Spirit's work:

> Now, this is his own great love and infinite condescension. He willingly proceeds or comes forth from the Father to be our comforter. He knew what we were, and what we could do, and what would be our dealings with him—he knew we

4 Owen, *Communion*, 411.

would grieve him, provoke him, quench his motions, defile his dwelling-place; and yet he would come to be our comforter.[5]

We've spent a lot of time looking at some of what the Holy Spirit does for us, but our goal is not merely to add to our understanding; we want to grow in our friendship and communion with the Spirit. And for that, we need to prepare our hearts not just to know but to delight in all that the Spirit does for us. What makes our understanding of the Spirit's work more delightful is knowing that he does it all freely and in love. When our hearts are able to see just how little we deserve, how much we have received, and how free and gracious the Spirit is, we are primed for communion with him.

5   Owen, *Communion*, 410.

23

What Not to Do

WHEN IT COMES TO our ongoing friendship with God the Holy Spirit, his role is to comfort us in all our troubles. But as we know well by now, a relationship is a two-way street; that means that there is a role for us to play in the process. All that is left for us now is to think about what we need to do in order to enjoy and live out our communion. When the Bible gets specific on the topic, it actually tells us more about what *not* to do. So here are three things that we should avoid as we seek to enjoy communion with the Holy Spirit.

First, because he dwells in us, *we should not grieve the Spirit.* The reference here is to the apostle Paul's words in the book of Ephesians: "Do not grieve the Holy Spirit of God, by whom you were sealed for the day of redemption" (Eph. 4:30; cf. Isa. 63:10). As we think about what Paul is saying to the church, we need to step carefully so that we do not badly misunderstand him. The word *grieve* has the sense of causing someone to be sorrowful, so it seems that the apostle is telling the church not to make the Holy

Spirit sad. But we must insist that there is an important sense in which it is *impossible* for us (or anything) to cause the Spirit of God to be sorrowful. Because he is divine and lacking in nothing, he cannot be robbed of his happiness and joy. He is in no way influenced or disappointed by our actions, for that would imply weakness and changeability on his part. Simply put, you and I do not have the power to make the Spirit sad.

But if that's true, then what is Paul warning us against? Why is he telling us not to do something that is, in the end, impossible? Owen sees two truths at work in what Paul says. On one hand, we know that the Spirit loves us and wants what is best for us. He cares deeply about us as a good, tender, and kind friend. And like any friend, he is not pleased when we make foolish choices and engage in self-destructive behaviors. That's the opposite of what he wants for us.

On the other hand, whatever Paul means by grieving the Spirit, it must be related to his work of making us holy. In Ephesians 4, the apostle Paul urges the church both to put off certain sinful behaviors that characterized their life before Christ and to put on attitudes and actions that are consistent with their new spiritual life. It is in that context that the command comes to us, so we can best understand that what Paul means by *grieving* the Spirit is not making him sad, but living a life devoted to something other than the holiness he brings to his people. Not grieving the Spirit requires us to live holy lives, both avoiding sin and cultivating godly virtues. When you take time to ponder the love and kindness of the Spirit, and when that consideration motivates you to avoid sin and walk in holiness, you are in that moment living out and enjoying friendship with God the Spirit.

When we fail to shape our lives around the love and care of the Spirit, we lose the power for and joy in obedience that we were meant to have. When his kindness and comfort mean little to us, then obedience will either be a burden or absent altogether. Owen suggests that we have a conversation like this with our souls:

> The Holy Ghost, in his infinite love and kindness toward me, has condescended to be my comforter; he does it willingly, freely, powerfully. What have I received from him! In the multitude of my perplexities [struggles] how has he refreshed my soul! Can I live one day without his consolations? And shall I be regardless of him in that wherein he is concerned? Shall I grieve him by negligence, sin, and folly? Shall not his love constrain me to walk before him to all well-pleasing?[1]

When we strive to avoid grieving the Spirit, we are enjoying fellowship with him.

Second, because the Holy Spirit is powerfully at work in us, *we should not quench (or extinguish) the Spirit.* Here the emphasis is less on how we treat and respect the Holy Spirit himself and more on how we treat his work. We might *grieve* the Spirit as he is a person living in us, but when we *quench* the Spirit, we are stifling his activity in us.

Think of all the ways we have seen that the Spirit is at work in our lives. He strives to produce the fruit of godliness (Gal. 5:22–25), to convince us of God's love (Rom. 5:5), and to

---

1 John Owen, *Communion with the Triune God*, ed. Kelly M. Kapic and Justin Taylor (Wheaton, IL: Crossway, 2007), 415.

empower us to serve and build up the church (1 Cor. 12:7). He stirs up the grace of Christ in us and brings us fresh supplies of grace in our time of need. All this work of the Spirit is like a burning fire in our soul, which we want to continue growing throughout our lives.

Quenching the Spirit, then, is like throwing a soaking wet log onto the fire of his work in us. But that raises the question, What does it look like to quench the Spirit? Surely we want to be wary of doing any such thing, so it makes sense to be clear about what we should be avoiding. Owen summarizes the meaning of Paul's warning in this way: "Take heed . . . lest, by the power of your lusts and temptations, you attend [pay attention] not to his workings, but hinder him in his goodwill towards you."[2] When we live our lives without any awareness of the Spirit's work in us, or when we care infinitely more about the things of our daily lives than what he wants to produce in us, or when we do things we know are exactly the opposite of what the Spirit desires for us, then we are quenching his work. Again, it's like throwing a wet log onto a fire; it won't put it out, but it will reduce the blaze.

Instead of quenching the Spirit through sin or failure to pay careful attention, we should "fan into flame the gift of God" (2 Tim. 1:6). We do this by something the Puritans called "improving" the Spirit's work and gifts. The idea is not that there is something wrong with the Spirit's work so that we need to make it better, but rather that we ought carefully and watchfully to put his gifts to work in order to bear the good fruit for which they were given. By valuing the Spirit's love and being diligent to fight

2   Owen, *Communion*, 416.

sin, live righteously, and serve faithfully, we can make that fire burn stronger and stronger in our hearts. This is another crucial way that we experience communion with the Spirit.

Third, because the Spirit works through the preaching of his word, *we should not resist him.* In Acts 7, Stephen condemned his hearers, saying, "You always resist the Holy Spirit. As your fathers did, so do you" (Acts 7:51). They were guilty of resisting the Spirit because they had joined their fathers in persecuting and even killing the prophets (Acts 7:52). The Spirit's work is closely tied up in the proclamation of God's truth. Luke tells us that Stephen's opponents could not get the best of him because of the wisdom given to him by the Spirit to speak and proclaim the truth of Christ (Acts 6:10). In a similar way, Paul reminded the Corinthians that his proclamation of the gospel among them was attended by a "demonstration of the Spirit and of power" (1 Cor. 2:4), as evidenced by their conversion.

The prophets and apostles are no longer with us, but we have their words written down for us, and they are every bit as authoritative today as they were when they were first written or spoken. In our times, the work of the Spirit is in part to empower pastors and teachers to proclaim the word that he has inspired for the benefit and building up of believers in the church. This means that one of the key ways we live out our relationship with the Spirit is to listen humbly and reverently to the word as it is preached week in and week out by Spirit-empowered preachers in our churches. When we are inattentive to, disinterested in, or critical of the Bible as it is preached to us, we are resisting the Spirit. But when we give due honor to the preaching of his word, we are communing with the Holy Spirit.

All three of these warnings represent sins that believers must be on guard against and also ways that we can pursue a closer walk with the Spirit—these are real dangers and real opportunities for fellowship with the Spirit. Because he is dwelling in us, we should honor and cherish his presence; we must not grieve him. Because he is powerfully at work in us, we should fan his gift into flame; we must not quench him. Because he works through the proclamation of his word, we must listen expectantly; we must not resist him.

24

Worshiping the Spirit

IN THIS BOOK we largely have been considering each person of the Trinity on his own. The danger with that approach is that we might lose sight of the fact that the three persons of the Godhead—Father, Son, and Spirit—are also a perfect unity. This means "it is impossible to *worship any one person*, and not worship the *whole* Trinity."[1] This is not because the persons are identical to one another, but because they all share in the same divine essence. So when we praise God for his "infinite excellency, dignity, [and] majesty,"[2] all three persons are adored and worshiped.

With that said, it is important for the purposes of our relationship with the Spirit to recognize that believers can and should worship him directly. When we experience the comfort and love and grace and powerful help of the Spirit, it should stir us up to love, worship, pray to, and believe in him as our God. We don't

1 John Owen, *Communion with the Triune God*, ed. Kelly M. Kapic and Justin Taylor (Wheaton, IL: Crossway, 2007), 419.
2 Owen, *Communion*, 420.

need to worry, for this worship does not diminish or insult the Father and the Son in the least. This means that we should pay particular attention to the distinct things that the Spirit does for us so that we can worship and love him as we ought. Each one of the things the Spirit does in order to bring us comfort (e.g., convincing us of God's love, assuring us of our inheritance) should serve as fuel for our worship and love for him. Owen suggests four ways that we can particularly worship the Spirit.

First, *we should remember his kindness to us*. Oftentimes the Spirit comforts us, but we take no notice and refuse to be consoled; we grieve him. Other times we might enjoy his comfort but never stop to realize and appreciate that he is the one who brought it to us. We are so often clueless and distracted when our hearts should be singing:

> This [comfort] is from the Holy Ghost; he is the Comforter, the God of all consolations; I know there is no joy, peace, hope, nor comfort, but what he works, gives, and bestows. . . . What price, now, shall I set upon his love! How shall I value the mercy I have received![3]

The Spirit is so kind to us, even though we are so often unworthy and ungrateful.

Second, *we should praise and give thanks to him*. The Spirit is no less worthy of praise and honor than the Father and the Son; he is every bit as essential to our life and salvation as they are. If we praise the Father for setting his love on us and the Son for re-

3 Owen, *Communion*, 422.

deeming us by his death and resurrection, shouldn't we also praise and glorify the Holy Spirit for his work in bringing us comfort? When we experience the joy, peace, and growth in obedience he brings, our hearts should be moved to rejoice in him and praise his name. This sense of delight in and thankfulness for the work of the Spirit is an important way we live out our friendship with him; it is how we respond to his presence in us.

Third, *we should pray to the Spirit*, asking him for the assistance and comfort he brings. When we consider how badly we need his help, what amazing privileges he brings to us, and the fact that he is sovereign in the way he gives his gifts, we will find ourselves motivated to pray to him! It is particularly in prayer that "we meet him, his love, grace, and authority," and so prayer to the Spirit is "the daily work of believers. They look upon, and by faith consider, the Holy Ghost as promised to be sent. In this promise, they know, lies all their grace, peace, mercy, joy, and hope."[4]

Fourth, *we should confess our sins against the Spirit*. Friends sometimes wrong each other, so a healthy relationship requires both the ability to apologize for our faults and to extend forgiveness when wronged. And despite our best intentions, our words, actions, and attitudes sometimes grieve the Spirit, quench his work, and resist his word. This fact ought to create a godly sorrow in us, not because we are fearful of God's judgment and wrath, but rather because we love the Spirit and are saddened to find ourselves being unloving friends. Thankfully, the Spirit is a good friend to us; he is faithful and loving even when we are not. When we confess our sins against him, he assures us of his kindness and forgiveness.

4 Owen, *Communion*, 423.

If you want to grow in your love for and worship of the Holy Spirit, just consider for a moment how terrible it would be to live without his ministry of comfort and love. People who do not know the Lord Jesus and who have not received the Spirit from the Father must bear their burdens and wrestle with their troubles on their own. They have no indwelling help and consolation but are left to their own devices.

Now, it is true that many people who do not have the Spirit of God seem to navigate their lives without any noticeable lack of peace. I know unbelievers who seem to have far less trouble and far more daily ease than I do. They've got all the money, health, success, and leisure that a human being could want. But when I look closely, this happiness is usually shallow. When trials inevitably come—and in a life that always ends in the grave, they will surely come—there is nothing and no one to comfort a human soul at the deepest level other than the Spirit of God. This doesn't mean that unbelievers cannot bear up under their troubles with something like poise and grace, but it is a peace that is largely external. Self-discipline and a desire to be strong can carry someone along for some time, but putting on a brave face and posting inspirational pictures on social media is a pale imitation of the comfort the Spirit brings to us.

In fact, apart from the Holy Spirit, all our personal strength and resolve is actually working against our best interests. When people learn to cope with tragedy and difficulty apart from God's Spirit, they are actually "striving to be quiet under that which God sent on purpose to disturb them."[5] In his kindness, God

5   Owen, *Communion*, 424.

sometimes sends difficulties and sorrows in order to show people that they are not okay, that something is wrong, that they are not right with God, and that this world is not heaven. But those who have learned to crank up their self-discipline and deal patiently with their pain apart from the Spirit are actually failing to learn the lesson that God intends for them. How much better is the comfort of the Holy Spirit than anything we can produce in our own strength!

Consider also that apart from the Spirit, men and women have no peace. Their God-given conscience condemns them, so their souls will be plagued by guilt and a sense of impending judgment. Again, this is meant to drive people to the Lord for forgiveness and mercy, but instead many people find ways to quiet their conscience: by doing good works, by participating in various religious activities, or (perhaps most commonly) by simply assuring themselves that they are "good people." In the end, those are all pale and sad imitations of genuine peace with God. When these people stand before God's judgment, they will find that he never agrees to their terms of peace.

There is no true, saving religion apart from the Holy Spirit. People might say they are Christians. Maybe they grew up in a church-going home or once prayed a prayer and invited Jesus into their hearts. But "if the Spirit dwells not in you, if he be not your Comforter, neither is God your Father, nor the Son your Advocate, nor have you any portion in the gospel."[6] Unless we have the Spirit, our joy will lack any sure foundation, and our hope will prove to be false.

6 Owen, *Communion*, 426.

All of this should move us to worship and delight in God the Holy Spirit. Think for a moment about how easily our hearts are moved to rejoice in things that are of limited value—a promotion at work, a victory by our favorite sports team, a new car. How much easier should it be for our hearts to praise the Holy Spirit? After all, he is the one who gives spiritual life to those the Father has loved. He causes us to be born again, grants us repentance and faith, and unites us to Christ, applying all the benefits of his death and resurrection to us. He is the one who lovingly comes to dwell in unworthy and ungrateful people like you and me. He gives us comfort in our griefs and strength in our trials. He assures us of God's love, gives us a desire for holiness, and is the guarantee of our eternal hope. How could we not love a friend like him?

Conclusion

I'M STRUCK BY how well Owen's work stands the test of time. He seems to have anticipated the two common ways that we reduce the Christian faith to something far less than it was intended to be. On the one hand, there is a popular way of talking about Christianity today that makes it seem as if it were almost completely a matter of doctrinal knowledge, as if our friendship with God is lived out in the memorization of catechisms and in the believing of as many true things about him as possible. On the other hand, it is also common to talk about the faith in a way that reduces it to mere emotion and sentimentality, as if God doesn't care what you believe so long as you're excited about him.

Communion with God seems to be an antidote perfectly designed for what plagues us. Owen's biblical vision for the Christian life is warm-blooded, passionate, and full of emotion. But for those feelings to be genuinely pleasing to God, they must be moved not by anything in us or even by a vague sense of God's power and goodness. Rather, it is the truths on display in the gospel—the stunning love of the Father, the incredible grace of the Lord Jesus, the wonderful comfort of the Holy Spirit—that move our hearts to worship and delight in him. In Owen's understanding, you don't fully understand any point of Christian doctrine until it leads you into a closer and happier relationship with your God.

In fact, the only thing that I would add to Owen's work (if the ant can be so bold as to offer the elephant some advice) would be an emphasis on the way that our relationship with God is related to our involvement in a local church. It's not that this concept is altogether absent in Owen's thinking; he discusses how participating in the Lord's Supper and hearing the preaching of God's word are essential to our communion with the triune God. Rather, I think that Owen didn't emphasize this topic because he simply could not anticipate the way that commitment to and involvement in a local church is considered optional by many Christians today.

This is not how it was meant to be. Most of the New Testament is written to churches, not individuals. The idea is that God's people are meant to live out their relationship with God together, serving one another in the power of the Spirit and helping one another to walk with him more closely. Whatever growth you experience and whatever communion you enjoy in your personal life are meant to flow out of you to the benefit of your brothers and sisters in the church. So allow me to conclude by urging you to joyfully live out your friendship with God, but don't do it alone. Gather with your local church and commune with the Lord together until all his people are gathered together to live and be with him forever.

General Index

Scripture Index

Also Available from Crossway

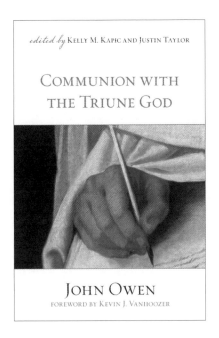